I0500433

Congressional
Research
Service

"Dirty Bombs": Technical Background, Attack Prevention and Response, Issues for Congress

Jonathan Medalia
Specialist in Nuclear Weapons Policy

June 24, 2011

Congressional Research Service

7-5700

www.crs.gov

R41890

CRS Report for Congress ———————————

Prepared for Members and Committees of Congress

Summary

Congress has long sought, through legislation and oversight, to protect the United States against terrorist threats, especially from chemical, biological, radiological, and nuclear (CBRN) weapons. Radiological dispersal devices (RDDs) are one type of CBRN weapon. Explosive-driven "dirty bombs" are an often-discussed type of RDD, though radioactive material can also be dispersed in other ways. This report provides background for understanding the RDD threat and responses, and presents issues for Congress.

Radioactive material is the necessary ingredient for an RDD. This material is composed of atoms that decay, emitting radiation. Some types and amounts of radiation are harmful to human health.

Terrorists have shown some interest in RDDs. They could use them in an attempt to disperse radioactive material to cause panic, area denial, and economic dislocation. While RDDs would be far less harmful than nuclear weapons, they are much simpler to build and the needed materials are used worldwide. Accordingly, some believe terrorists would be more likely to use RDDs than nuclear weapons. Key points include:

- RDDs could contaminate areas with radioactive material, increasing long-term cancer risks, but would probably kill few people promptly. Nuclear weapons could destroy much of a city, kill tens of thousands of people, and contaminate much larger areas with fallout.

- Cleanup cost after an RDD attack could range from less than a billion dollars to tens of billions of dollars, depending on area contaminated, decontamination technologies used, and level of cleanup required.

- Terrorists would face obstacles to using RDDs, such as obtaining materials, designing an effective weapon, and avoiding detection.

Governments and organizations have taken steps to prevent an RDD attack. Domestically, the Nuclear Regulatory Commission has issued regulations to secure radioactive sources. The Department of Homeland Security develops and operates equipment to detect radioactive material. The National Nuclear Security Administration (NNSA) has recovered thousands of disused or abandoned sources. Some state and local governments have taken steps to prepare for an RDD attack. Internationally, the International Atomic Energy Agency has led efforts to secure radioactive sources. Its Code of Conduct on the Safety and Security of Radioactive Sources offers guidance for protecting sources. The G8 Global Partnership has secured sources in Russia and elsewhere. A State Department program strengthens border security. Other nations and non-governmental organizations have acted to secure sources as well. Key points include:

- Nuclear Regulatory Commission actions have done much to instill a security culture for U.S. licensees of radioactive sources post-9/11.

- Many programs have sought to improve the security of radioactive sources overseas, but some incidents raise questions about security.

Should prevention fail, federal, state, and local governments have taken many measures to respond to and recover from an RDD attack. The National Response Framework "establishes a comprehensive, national, all-hazards approach to domestic incident response." The federal government has resources for recovery. Key points include:

- Government agencies have done much to prepare for and recover from an RDD attack. This work would help cope with other disasters. Conversely, planning for other disasters would help in the event of an RDD attack.

- Some experts have raised questions about the effectiveness of planning to respond to and recover from an RDD attack.

This report raises several issues for Congress, including:

- the priority for countering RDDs vs. other CBRN;

- the priority given to securing domestic vs. overseas radioactive sources;

- whether to establish a radiation detection system in cities;

- how best to prepare for decontamination following an RDD attack;

- how to dispose of potentially large volumes of waste generated by decontamination;

- whether to modify certain personnel reliability standards;

- whether to modify the pace of a program for implementing certain security enhancements for U.S. radioactive sources; and

- how to improve radiological forensics capability.

CRS Report R41891, *"Dirty Bombs": Background in Brief*, by Jonathan Medalia, is an abridged version of this report.

Contents

Figures

Tables

Appendixes

Contacts

Introduction

In one nightmare scenario, a terrorist "dirty bomb" spreads radioactive material across dozens of square miles, causing panic in the target area and beyond, costing tens of billions of dollars to remediate, costing further sums in lost wages and business, compelling the demolition and rebuilding of contaminated buildings, forcing difficult decisions on how to dispose of contaminated rubble and decontamination chemicals, and requiring people to relocate from areas with elevated levels of radiation.

But in other scenarios, a terrorist plot fails. Security measures keep terrorists from obtaining radioactive material. Terrorists use a weakly radioactive material that causes little contamination. They obtain too little material to be effective, or so much that it kills them before they could attack. Equipment detects the material overseas, at U.S. borders, or inside the United States. Material disperses over a small area, facilitating cleanup, or so widely that much of the area would not require decontamination. Some blows out to sea. Such factors as weather, form of material, and degree of remediation required affect cleanup cost by several orders of magnitude and greatly reduce the damage that terrorists could expect to cause. Terrorist awareness of such failure paths might deter an attack.

Radiological dispersal devices (RDDs) may be explosive-driven—a dirty bomb—or use nonexplosive means like a crop duster airplane. Radioactive material may be dispersed indoors to contaminate a building, though the scenario most commonly discussed involves detonation of a dirty bomb outdoors. Because of their potential disruptive effects, legislation includes RDDs as one type of weapon of mass destruction (WMD), along with chemical, biological, and nuclear weapons,[1] and a U.N. commission in 1948 included "radio active material weapons" as a form of WMD.[2] Congress has been deeply involved in efforts to protect the United States and other nations against terrorist attacks, especially since 9/11.

The large range of possible effects of radiation results in widespread misunderstanding of the characteristics and effects of RDDs, especially when augmented by fear of radiation that has existed for over a half-century. To address these and related problems, this report provides background on RDDs and issues they raise; it does not track policy actions concerning RDDs in detail. It attempts to help understanding of these weapons in order to aid Congress in its oversight and funding of programs to counter them.[3] Understanding the threat that an RDD attack poses

---

[1] The Intelligence Reform and Terrorism Prevention Act of 2004, P.L. 108-458, includes these four types of weapons in its definition of weapons of mass destruction; see 6 U.S.C. 485 (a) (6).

[2] Commission for Conventional Armaments, resolution defining armaments, U.N. doc. S/C.3/30, adopted at the 13th meeting of the Commission for Conventional Armaments, August 12, 1948, in U.S. Department of State *Bulletin*, August 29, 1948, p. 268.

[3] Useful documents on RDDs include Roger Eckhardt, "Ionizing Radiation—It's Everywhere," *Los Alamos Science*, no. 23, 1995, http://www.fas.org/sgp/othergov/doe/lanl/00326627.pdf; Charles Ferguson et al., *Commercial Radioactive Sources: Surveying the Security Risks*, Center for Nonproliferation Studies, January 2003; U.S. Nuclear Regulatory Commission, "Medical, Industrial, and Academic Uses of Nuclear Materials," http://www.nrc.gov/ materials/medical.html; Gregory Van Tuyle et al., "Reducing RDD Concerns Related to Large Radiological Source Applications," September 2003, http://www.nti.org/e_research/official_docs/labs/LAUR03-6%202.pdf; Peter Zimmerman with Cheryl Loeb, "Dirty Bombs: The Threat Revisited," *Defense Horizons*, January 2004, pp. 1-11, http://www.hps.org/documents/RDD_report.pdf; Charles Ferguson and William Potter, *The Four Faces of Nuclear Terrorism*, Monterey, CA, Center for Nonproliferation Studies, 2004; Argonne National Laboratory, "Radiological Dispersal Device (RDD)," Human Health Fact Sheet, August 2005, http://www.ead.anl.gov/pub/doc/rdd.pdf; K.G. (continued...)

---

and—of equal importance—the limits of that threat requires a brief discussion of the relevant science. Subsequent sections of this report turn to RDDs, preventing an attack, and response to and recovery from an attack. This report then offers observations and issues and options for Congress. It compares RDDs and nuclear weapons but does not address chemical or biological weapons. It is not intended as a comprehensive summary of the many domestic and international programs that address the RDD threat in some way.

Overview: Congress and "Dirty Bombs"

Congress has demonstrated a sustained interest in the threat that RDDs pose to the United States and other nations. It has enacted legislation pertaining to RDDs, held hearings on them, and requested numerous reports from the Government Accountability Office (GAO). It has done so for a number of reasons. Radioactive materials are used worldwide for medical, industrial, research, and other beneficial purposes. Yet their security is far from airtight, especially in foreign countries, as evidenced by many reports of trafficking and attempted trafficking. Terrorists could create an RDD, though not necessarily an effective one, by stealing radioactive material and detonating an explosive charge next to it. Preventing an RDD attack and preparing to respond to and recover from an attack are thus matters of homeland security.

Terrorists, too, are interested in RDDs. An RDD has the potential to contaminate some square miles (ranging from less than one to perhaps 100, depending on how one defines contamination) with radioactive material. The attack could render an area off-limits for days to years, cause significant economic disruption (e.g., by forcing the closure of a port or evacuating the center of a city), cost tens of billions of dollars to remediate, impose further costs in lost wages and business, force the demolition and rebuilding of contaminated streets and buildings, increase the cancer rate over the long term, and cause panic and a climate of fear in the target area and far beyond.

Despite the seeming ease of launching a successful RDD attack, terrorists have not done so. The reasons are necessarily speculative, but may include difficulties in handling radioactive material, lack of sufficient expertise to fabricate material into an effective weapon, a shift to smaller-scale but simpler attacks using standard weapons and explosives, and improved security.

Of course, such factors cannot guarantee that no attack will occur. Accordingly, the executive branch, with congressional support and sometimes at congressional direction, has undertaken many measures to reduce the likelihood of an attack. These include increasing the security of radioactive material, augmenting counterterrorism efforts by intelligence and law enforcement agencies, conducting "stings" to catch would-be terrorists attempting to purchase radioactive material and those willing to sell it, and deploying radiation detectors worldwide. The government has also made extensive plans for responding to and recovering from an attack. Foreign governments and international organizations have taken similar measures, and some nongovernmental organizations have provided resources and analysis in support of counter-RDD efforts.

(...continued)

Andersson et al., "Estimation of Health Hazards Resulting from a Radiological Terrorist Attack in a City," *Radiation Protection Dosimetry,* vol. 131, no. 3 (2008), pp. 297-307, http://rpd.oxfordjournals.org/content/131/3/297 full; and John Poston, Sr., et al., *Management of Terrorist Events Involving Radioactive Material,* report 138, National Council on Radiation Protection & Measurement, 2001, summary at http://www.ncrppublications.org/Reports/138.

The prospect of an RDD attack raises several issues for Congress, including:

- the priority to be given to countering terrorism using RDDs vs. other types of unconventional weapons;

- the priority to be given to domestic vs. overseas expenditures to secure radioactive sources;

- whether to use federal funds to develop and deploy radiation detection networks in major cities and elsewhere;

- how best to prepare for decontamination following an RDD attack, such as the balance between R&D, stockpiling of equipment and supplies, training, rapid distribution of information, and analysis of the cost of decontamination vs. demolition and reconstruction;

- how to dispose of contaminated waste, including rubble from demolition and chemicals from decontamination, following an attack;

- whether to modify standards for permitting unescorted access to certain U.S. radioactive sources;

- whether to modify the pace of a program for implementing certain security enhancements for U.S. radioactive sources; and

- how to enhance U.S. capability for radiological forensics.

A Note on Terminology

Legislation, media reports, and the public use the term "weapon of mass destruction," or "WMD," extensively to refer to chemical, biological, radiological, and nuclear (CBRN) weapons. The term "WMD" is problematic from an analytic perspective, however, in that it lumps these unconventional weapons together and implies that they are similar even though each type differs greatly from the others in its mechanisms and effects. As a result, significantly different approaches are required to address the threats that each type poses. The term is also unclear. For example, does "destruction" refer to number of people killed, buildings destroyed, or economic damage? If the reference is to number of people killed, the various types of "WMD" would differ immensely. If "mass" refers to number of people killed, how many people constitute "mass"? If a biological weapon killed five people, as the anthrax attacks did in 2001, would that weapon count as a weapon of mass destruction, or would the threshold be, say, 5,000? As a result of these difficulties, many analyses, and this report, refer instead to "CBRN," which explicitly states the types of weapons meant and avoids defining "mass" and "destruction."

Efforts to Negotiate a Radiological Weapons Convention

During World War II, in addition to developing nuclear weapons, the Manhattan Project considered the direct use of radiological materials as a weapon. This concept of a "radiological weapon" (RW) is the same as that of a radiological dispersal device (RDD). Development work on RWs continued after the war. During the Korean War, proposals were advanced for laying down a barrier of radioactive material along the Chinese border, but RW development appears to have ended by the mid-1950s.

In 1976, the Ford Administration identified the use of radioactive materials as a potential terrorist threat, and began discussions with the Soviet Union to ban RWs and the use of radioactive materials in war even if not weaponized. In 1979, the United States and Soviet Union tabled elements of an RW Convention at the Committee on Disarmament, and in 1983 the renamed Conference on Disarmament (CD) began multilateral negotiations on the Convention. In its 1983 report to the U.N. General Assembly, the CD included a draft RW Convention, with some provisions still to be agreed. Negotiations were hampered by the issue of attacks on nuclear facilities. At least one delegation, Sweden, considered this issue more important than radiological weapons, and gave little support to the Convention. Further, when the CD's 1984 session began, the Reagan Administration declined to actively pursue the negotiations because of a concern that a convention might be seen as controlling nuclear weapons. The RW issue remains on the CD's agenda as part of the item "New types of weapons of mass destruction and new systems of such weapons; radiological weapons." However, it has not been accorded a high priority, and the CD is no closer to concluding a Convention, or resolving the issue of attacks on nuclear facilities, than it was in 1983.

Provided by Pierce S. Corden, former RW lead officer on the U.S. CD Delegation, and currently a Visiting Scholar, Center for Science, Technology and Security Policy, American Association for the Advancement of Science, February 17, 2011.

Radiation and Radiological Dispersal Devices

Radiation and Its Effects

This section provides a brief technical background; readers seeking detail should read **Appendix A** instead. Many atoms are stable: they will remain in their current form indefinitely. Some atoms are unstable, or radioactive. They "decay" or "disintegrate," usually into atoms of a different element, often through emission of various particles.[4] Decay is often accompanied by emission of gamma rays, a form of electromagnetic radiation, often of high energy. A radioactive atom is called a "radionuclide"; that term refers to properties of individual atoms, while "radioactive material" refers to bulk properties. Each radionuclide decays in a specific way. For example, when uranium-235 decays, it emits alpha particles and gamma rays, mainly of low energy; cobalt-60 emits beta particles and high-energy gamma rays when it decays. A unit called the curie (Ci) measures radioactivity; $1 \text{ Ci} = 3.7 \times 10^{10}$ disintegrations per second.[5] The time in which half the atoms of a mass of a radioactive material decay is called the half-life.

Radiation strikes people constantly, but much of it, like light or radio waves, is harmless or nearly so. Some high-energy radiation is "ionizing." Most atoms have no net electrical charge because they have an equal number of positively-charged protons and negatively-charged electrons. Ionizing radiation knocks electrons off atoms, turning atoms into positively-charged ions that damage living cells. Very low doses of radiation produce few if any effects, but progressively higher doses may increase the risk of cancer or may cause radiation sickness or death. Effects

---

[4] The most common types of particles emitted in decay are alpha particles (two protons plus two neutrons), beta particles (an electron or positron, with the latter being a positively-charged electron), and, for heavy elements, neutrons.

[5] The International System of Units uses a different unit, the becquerel (Bq), where 1 Bq = 1 disintegration per second.

visible in individuals, such as nausea, are "deterministic"; their severity varies with dose. Effects detectable in populations, such as increased incidence of cancer, are "stochastic"; their probability varies with dose. In the United States, dose is usually measured in units of rem.[6] This unit takes into account the amount of radiation absorbed and its biological effects. The average dose for the U.S. population is estimated at 620 millirem (mrem; 1,000 mrem = 1 rem) per year, about half from medical sources and half from natural background.[7] An RDD attack is likely to expose few people to a dose of more than a few rem per year, even using the unrealistic assumption that they remain in the affected area without sheltering for a year.

Any effects from a dose of a few rem per year are likely to be stochastic. Views differ on the harm from that dose. One view is that any amount of radiation increases cancer risk; another is that there is no evidence that radiation of less than about 10 rem per year increases that risk. The U.S. Nuclear Regulatory Commission (NRC) uses the former approach to be conservative in setting dose standards.[8] Further, various standards imply different degrees of harm from a dose of a few rem per year. For dose to the public resulting from the nuclear fuel cycle (e.g., nuclear power plants), the Environmental Protection Agency uses a standard of 25 mrem per year of whole-body dose.[9] NRC adopts that standard,[10] and in addition has a dose standard of 100 mrem per year for members of the public from operations licensed by NRC.[11] That agency also has established an occupational dose limit of 5 rem per year.[12] The occupational dose limit in Japan was reportedly 10 rem per year, a figure raised to 25 rem per year in the wake of the Fukushima Daiichi incident.[13] According to one expert, doses greater than 25 rem are often received in a short period of time, producing deterministic effects, the severity of which increases with dose.[14] As the foregoing discussion shows, there is no single level that marks the line between an acceptable and unacceptable dose.

An RDD attack would elevate dose in the affected area beyond background. The Environmental Protection Agency (EPA) issued guidance in 1991 for protective actions following nuclear and radiological incidents except nuclear war, and the Federal Emergency Management Agency (FEMA) issued guidance in 2008 for protection and recovery following RDD and improvised nuclear device (IND, i.e., a terrorist-made nuclear weapon) incidents.[15] [16] Both agencies

---

[6] The International System of Units, used widely outside the United States, uses a different unit, the sievert (Sv), where 1 Sv = 100 rem, and 1 millisievert (mSv) = 0.1 rem.

[7] National Council on Radiation Protection and Measurement, *Ionizing Radiation Exposure of the Population of the United States,* report 160 (2009), available through http://www ncrppublications.org/Reports/160. The figure of 620 mrem (6.2 millisievert) is from the council's webpage "NCRP Report No. 160 Section 1 Pie Chart," http://www.ncrponline.org/Publications/160_Pie_charts-Sec1.html, and the pie chart showing the contribution of various sources of radiation to dose is at http://www.ncrponline.org/images/160_pie_charts/Fig1-1.pdf.

[8] U.S. Nuclear Regulatory Commission. "Fact Sheet on Biological Effects of Radiation," http://www nrc.gov/reading-rm/doc-collections/fact-sheets/bio-effects-radiation html.

[9] 10 CFR 190.10(a).

[10] 20 CFR 1301(e).

[11] 20 CFR 1301(a)(1).

[12] 20 CFR 1201(a)(1)(i).

[13] Keith Bradsher and Hiroko Tabuchi, "Last Defense at Troubled Reactors: 50 Japanese Workers," *New York Times,* March 16, 2011, p. 1.

[14] Dade Moeller, *Environmental Health,* revised edition (Cambridge, Harvard University Press, 1997), p. 250.

[15] U.S. Environmental Protection Agency. Office of Radiation Programs. *Manual of Protective Action Guides and Protective Actions for Nuclear Incidents,* revised 1991 (second printing, May 1992), http://www.epa.gov/radiation/docs/er/400-r-92-001.pdf; and Federal Emergency Management Agency, "Planning Guidance for Protection and (continued...)

---

recommended "protective action guides" (PAGs). A PAG is "the projected dose to a reference individual, from an accidental or deliberate release of radioactive material, at which a specific protective action to reduce or avoid that dose is recommended. Thus, protective actions are designed to be taken before the anticipated dose is realized."[17] PAGs provide guidance on emergency actions like sheltering in place or evacuation.

FEMA divides the incident response into three phases. The early phase starts "at the beginning of the incident when immediate decisions for effective protective actions are required, and when actual field measurement data generally are not available." The beginning is not necessarily clear. While an explosive-driven dirty bomb would announce its presence, FEMA observes that "in the event of a covert dispersal, discovery or detection may not occur for days or weeks."[18] For the early phase, for a PAG of 1 to 5 rem, the protective action recommendation is sheltering in place or evacuation.[19] The intermediate phase after an attack "is usually assumed to begin after the incident source and releases have been brought under control and protective action decisions can be made based on measurements of exposure and radioactive materials that have been deposited."[20] For that phase, FEMA recommends "relocation of the public" for a projected dose of 2 rem for the first year and 0.5 rem per year for any subsequent year.[21][22] PAGs assume that a person is in the affected area, unprotected, 24 hours a day, 7 days a week, for the entire period. This is unrealistic; sheltering and cleanup would reduce dose below the assumed level in the event of an RDD attack. The late phase starts when recovery and cleanup begin, and ends when such actions have been completed. FEMA does not have a PAG for the late phase because it would not be an emergency situation and because authorities would need to optimize among many factors (economic, land use, technical feasibility, etc.) in determining which areas need to be remediated to what levels.

As a guide to quantities of material that should be protected, in 2003 the International Atomic Energy Agency (IAEA) revised its Code of Conduct on the Safety and Security of Radioactive Sources.[23] The IAEA decided that the code "should serve as guidance to States for—*inter alia*—the development and harmonization of policies, laws and regulations on the safety and security of radioactive sources."[24] It lists 16 radionuclides that are in common use and could pose a threat. For each radionuclide, the code lists three categories of radiation and the threshold radiation value for each category based on potential to cause deterministic effects. Category 1 sources are those

---

(...continued)

Recovery Following Radiological Dispersal Device (RDD) and Improvised Nuclear Device (IND) Incidents," 73 *Federal Register* 45029-45048, August 1, 2008.

[16] The U.S. Centers for Disease Control and Prevention offers a guide to personal protection in the event of an RDD attack, "Frequently Asked Questions (FAQs) About Dirty Bombs," http://emergency.cdc.gov/radiation/dirtybombs.asp.

[17] Federal Emergency Management Agency, "Planning Guidance for Protection and Recovery Following Radiological Dispersal Device (RDD) and Improvised Nuclear Device (IND) Incidents," 73 *Federal Register*, August 1, 2008, p. 45034.

[18] Ibid., p. 45032.

[19] Ibid., pp. 45032, 45035.

[20] Ibid., p. 45032.

[21] Ibid., p. 45035.

[22] The levels selected for PAGs were controversial. Some felt that PAG dose levels could be applied to situations other than a nuclear or RDD attack, supplanting standards that set dose at lower levels, which "could lead to dramatically weakened public protections." Douglas Guarino, "Obama Team to Review Contentious Bush EPA Nuclear Emergency Guide," *InsideEPA.com,* January 26, 2009.

[23] International Atomic Energy Agency, *Code of Conduct on the Safety and Security of Radioactive Sources,* January 2004, http://www.iaea.org/Publications/Booklets/RadioactiveSources/radioactivesource.pdf.

[24] International Atomic Energy Agency, *Code of Conduct on the Safety and Security of Radioactive Sources,* p. 2.

that, if not safely managed or securely protected, could cause permanent injury to someone who handled them for a few minutes, and death to someone who handled them unshielded for a few minutes to an hour. For Category 2 sources, the corresponding figures are minutes to hours and hours to days. Category 3 sources, if not safely managed or securely protected, could cause injury to someone handling them for some hours.[25]

NRC found, "Of the 16 radionuclides, only four are widely used in civilian applications in this country: Cobalt-60, cesium-137, iridium-192, and americium-241."[26] An expert panel highlighted the risk from cesium-137 chloride:

> Because of its dispersibility, solubility, penetrating radiation, source activity, and presence across the United States in facilities such as hospitals, blood banks, and universities, many of which are located in large population centers, radioactive cesium chloride is a greater concern than other Category 1 and 2 sources for some attack scenarios. This concern is exacerbated by the lack of an avenue for permanent disposal of high-activity cesium radiation sources, which can result in disused cesium sources sitting in licensees' storage facilities. As such, these sources pose unique risks.[27]

The Energy Policy Act of 2005 (P.L. 109-58, Section 651 (d)) mandates certain security measures for Category 1 and 2 sources as defined by the IAEA Code of Conduct. While the thresholds for the various categories in the code are based on the potential to cause deterministic effects, NRC considers Category 2 sources to be risk-significant: "The theft or diversion of risk-significant quantities of radioactive materials could lead to their use in a radiological dispersal device (RDD) or a radiological exposure device (RED)."[28] Since NRC judges that Category 2 sources could cause significant economic effects, the agency uses the lower threshold for Category 2 as the basis for mandating security measures beyond those in the Energy Policy Act.

Category 2 quantities are very small, often a fraction of a gram. For example, the quantity of concern for cesium-137 is 0.31 grams, which has 27 curies. Somewhat larger amounts can contaminate a substantial area. For example, 50 grams (1.8 ounces) of cesium-137 chloride would have about 1,000 curies. **Figure 1** models an RDD attack on Washington, DC, using 1,000 curies of this substance, which contaminates, to different levels, zones ranging in area from 0.81 to 5.10 square miles.

---

[25] Ibid., p. 15.

[26] "Prepared Statement of Robert J. Lewis," Director, Division of Materials Safety and State Agreements, Nuclear Regulatory Commission, in U.S. Congress. House. Committee on Homeland Security. Subcommittee on Emerging Threats, Cybersecurity, and Science and Technology, Status Report on Federal and Local Efforts to Secure Radiological Sources, field hearing, Brooklyn, NY, 111th Congress, 1st Session, serial no. 111-34, September 14, 2009, p. 21. The number following the name of the element represents the number of protons plus neutrons in the atom's nucleus.

[27] National Research Council. *Radiation Source Use and Replacement, Abbreviated Version*, p. 7.

[28] Nuclear Regulatory Commission, "Physical Protection of Byproduct Material: Proposed Rule," 75 *Federal Register* 33902, June 15, 2010. An RED would place radioactive material so as to expose people to radiation, rather than dispersing such material; see "RDDs and Nuclear Weapons."

Figure 1. A Possible RDD Attack on Washington, DC

Using 1,000 Curies of Cesium-137 Chloride

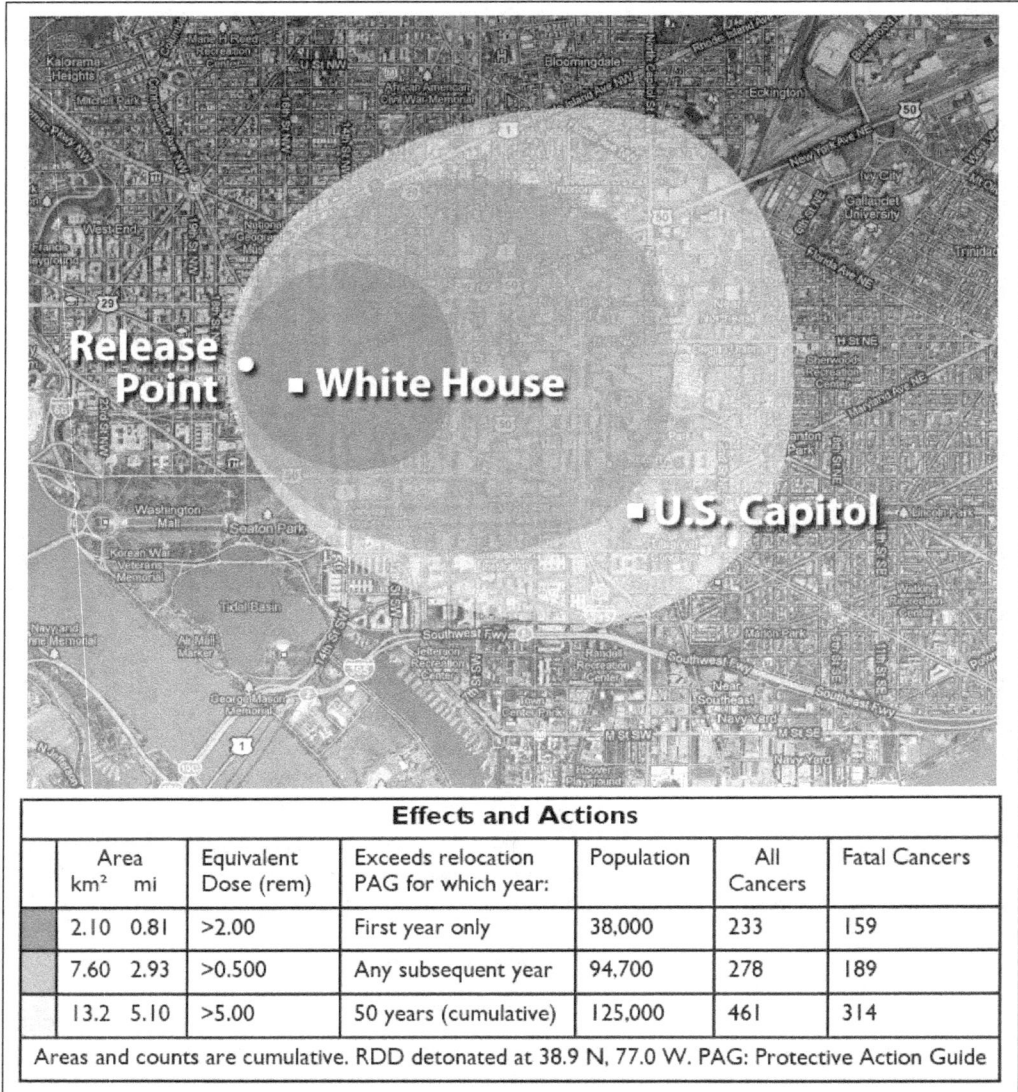

Effects and Actions						
	Area km² mi	Equivalent Dose (rem)	Exceeds relocation PAG for which year:	Population	All Cancers	Fatal Cancers
	2.10 0.81	>2.00	First year only	38,000	233	159
	7.60 2.93	>0.500	Any subsequent year	94,700	278	189
	13.2 5.10	>5.00	50 years (cumulative)	125,000	461	314
Areas and counts are cumulative. RDD detonated at 38.9 N, 77.0 W. PAG: Protective Action Guide						

Source: William Rhodes III, Senior Manager, International Security Systems Group, Sandia National Laboratories, September 2010; analysis by Heather Pennington; graphics by Mona Aragon.

Notes: (provided by William Rhodes): This map, based on an atmospheric dispersion model, shows where individuals are projected to have an increased risk of developing cancers due to radiation exposure over a year or more. The RDD in this scenario uses 1,000 curies of cesium-137 chloride (about 50 grams). The model assumes that all material used is dispersed, but that it is not dispersed evenly over the area. Wind is assumed to be from west to east at 7 mph. The model includes exposure from radioactive material both deposited on the surface and resuspended into the air and inhaled. EPA and FEMA have developed Protective Action Guides (PAGs) to indicate when long-term relocation of individuals should be considered. PAGs are primarily based on an assessment of the risk of developing cancer over an exposed individual's lifetime. They assume, conservatively, that individuals are unsheltered and remain in the area during the entire period described for each contour. Contours show where individuals, if not relocated per the PAG, are projected to receive at least a specified dose in a specified time, as follows: inner contour (red), dose in first year post-attack, >2.00 rem; middle contour (orange), dose in second year post-attack, >0.500 rem; and outer contour (yellow), cumulative dose in the first 50 years post-attack. >5.00 rem. The cigar-shaped plumes often seen in models of atmospheric dispersion occur for gases or very fine particles, which would be the case for chemical warfare agents or fallout from a nuclear weapon but not in the case depicted. Whether such plumes would occur for an RDD depends on such factors as wind speed, type of explosive, and particle size.

(Provided by CRS): This note compares lifetime incidence of, and deaths from, cancer to those resulting from the attack modeled in this Figure. For the United States, the lifetime risk of being diagnosed with cancer is 43.61 percent, and the lifetime risk of dying from cancer is 21.15 percent. (U.S. National Institutes of Health. National Cancer Institute. Surveillance Epidemiology and End Results (SEER). "SEER Cancer Statistics Review 1975-2007," Tables 1.14 and 1.17, http://seer.cancer.gov/csr/1975_2007/results_merged/topic_lifetime_risk.pdf) For the 125,000 people in the affected area, the estimated lifetime incidence of cancer would thus be approximately 54,513 people, and the estimated lifetime deaths from cancer, 26,438. The attack would increase the lifetime incidence of cancer by 461 people, and lifetime deaths from cancer by 314. The Figure assumes no relocation, sheltering, or decontamination. All these actions would occur in the real world, significantly reducing cancer incidence and deaths caused by the attack.

Might uranium or plutonium, the essential fuels of nuclear weapons, be used in an RDD? Technical experts rarely if ever consider uranium as an RDD material because the amount of radiation emitted per gram is extremely small, most of its gamma rays are of relatively low energy, and it poses less of a biological hazard than plutonium. Plutonium could be used in an RDD because of the biological hazards from alpha particles if inhaled. However, a terrorist group seeking materials for an RDD would probably find it easier to obtain radionuclides with common industrial uses; a terrorist group seeking to build a nuclear bomb would probably try to acquire uranium highly enriched in isotope 235 ("highly enriched uranium") rather than plutonium because only the former can be used in the simplest type of nuclear bomb; and a terrorist group seeking to build a nuclear bomb using plutonium would probably not squander any plutonium it acquired on an RDD. On the other hand, spent nuclear fuel, a highly radioactive mixture of many radionuclides including uranium and plutonium, could be used in an RDD.

RDDs and Nuclear Weapons

The type of RDD most commonly referenced in the press and in public discussion is the "dirty bomb," in which conventional explosives like dynamite disperse radioactive material, but a dirty bomb is only one type of RDD. There are other ways to disperse such material, such as placing it in traffic or dropping it from an airplane. Terrorists might also use a "radiological exposure device" (RED), in which radioactive material is placed (but not dispersed) so as to expose people to radiation. REDs would harm only people who remained near them for a length of time, and would contaminate little or no area; accordingly, they are of less concern than RDDs and this report makes only brief reference to them.

It is important to clear up a common misconception. The public and the media tend to lump nuclear weapons and RDDs together, probably because both involve radioactive materials.[29] However, the materials and processes used are very different, and so are the results. An RDD simply disperses radioactive material. The danger comes from radiation. The main physical effect of an effective RDD attack would be as an area denial weapon, contaminating perhaps several square miles to the extent that the affected population would have to relocate and requiring costly cleanup. An attack would likely have economic and psychological effects as well, but would cause no destruction (except that resulting from the explosion of a dirty bomb) and would

---

[29] This confusion may be beneficial. Uranium would have little physical effect if used in an RDD even though a certain form of uranium is suitable for a nuclear weapon. Yet James Cummings reportedly had acquired uranium in an apparent attempt to create an RDD. Walter Griffin, "Report: 'Dirty Bomb' Parts Found; Radioactive Materials Recovered from Home of Belfast [ME] Man Allegedly Slain by His Wife," *Bangor Daily News*, February 11, 2009.

probably kill few if any people promptly. A nuclear weapon uses uranium and plutonium, which are much less radioactive than the materials most effective in an RDD. The process is that fission and fusion of uranium, plutonium, and other materials release a vast amount of energy. The resulting explosion produces immediate blast and heat effects that can destroy a large part of a city and kill tens of thousands of people, and generates radioactive fallout whose impact would be felt over a longer term and a wider area. Estimates differ as to the area an RDD and a nuclear weapon would contaminate with radioactive material, depending on the height of burst of a nuclear weapon (and thus the quantity of material it lofted into the atmosphere that would become fallout), dispersibility of RDD material, wind patterns, radiation level at which an area is considered contaminated, and so on. A ground-burst nuclear weapon would contaminate a far larger area than an RDD.

While an attack using a nuclear weapon, such as a terrorist-made improvised nuclear device (IND), would be far more destructive, many see an RDD attack as more likely. It would be difficult for terrorists to make an IND on their own. They would need "special nuclear material" (SNM, mainly uranium highly enriched in isotope 235 or plutonium), which is heavily guarded, as well as extensive design work, precision equipment, and people with specialized skills. In contrast, radioactive materials that might be of use in an RDD are in use around the world, often in unguarded facilities. If terrorists obtained such material, they could disperse it using conventional explosives or other low-tech means. They could not manufacture the active materials for an IND or RDD, so would have to acquire them through other means.

Value of RDDs for Terrorists

An RDD's effects could meet multiple goals that terrorists might have. Effects include the following, listed here in the sequence in which they might occur:

- Prompt casualties, which would most likely come only from the explosion of a dirty bomb; many experts believe they would be few in number.[30]

- Panic. As an example of the panic potential of RDDs, a 2007 study by the University of Chicago's National Opinion Research Center found that 65 percent of urban residents said they would evacuate in the event of an RDD attack if the government made no recommendation on evacuation, and 39 percent said they would do so even if the government advised against evacuation.[31] Even an attack that released little radiation might cause panic.

- Economic disruption. If a port or city center were contaminated with radioactive material, commerce there might be suspended.

---

[30] Richard Meserve, former Chairman, Nuclear Regulatory Commission, held that an RDD might cause "deaths on the order of tens of people in most scenarios." U.S. Congress. Senate. Committee on Foreign Relations. *Dirty Bombs and Basement Nukes: The Terrorist Nuclear Threat,* hearing, 107th Congress, 2nd Session, 2002, p. 8.

[31] Michael Meit et al., *Spontaneous Evacuation Following a Dirty Bomb or Pandemic Influenza: Highlights from a National Survey of Urban Residents' Intended Behavior,* National Opinion Research Center, Walsh Center for Rural Health Analysis, Policy Analysis Brief, W Series, No. 12, Chicago, IL, and Bethesda, MD, November 2007, pp. 1-2, http://www.norc.org/nr/rdonlyres/7bebba5f-a019-4846-9885-3c7dc537e4ae/0/ spontaneousevacuationfollowingadirtybomborpandemicinfluenza.pdf.

- Asset denial. Public concern over the presence of radioactive material might lead people to abandon a building, subway system, or an area of a city for months to years.

- Decontamination, which might be done with chemicals or through demolition and reconstruction at a cost of billions of dollars.

- Long-term casualties resulting from exposure to or inhalation of radioactive material.

More speculatively, terrorists might see an RDD attack as an advertisement and a recruiting tool.

A 2007 study casts light on how an RDD attack might inflict economic damage and asset denial. The study analyzed RDD attacks on the ports of Los Angeles and Long Beach:

> Initial findings suggest that the chances of a successful dirty bomb attack are about 10–40% and that high radiological doses are confined to a relatively small area, limiting health effects to tens or at most hundreds of latent cancers, even with a major release. However, the economic consequences from a shutdown of the harbors due to the contamination could result in significant losses in the tens of billions of dollars, including the decontamination costs and the indirect economic impacts due to the port shutdown.[32]

Another study of the economic impacts of an attack on these ports using two RDDs assumed that the ports were shut for a month with no mitigation and no use of alternative ports. It placed the total U.S. losses at $8.5 billion for exports and $26.0 billion for imports.[33] An NNSA-sponsored study of the economic impacts of RDDs "modeled the impacts of four specific radioactive sources … Even without weaponization of the radioactive materials or optimization of the device the study found that the economic cost to the Nation could be in the billions of dollars. Costs included evacuation, relocation, clean-up, and lost wages."[34]

The Threat: Feasibility, Fear, Probability, Impediments

James Clapper, Director of National Intelligence, said in March 2011, "Some terror groups remain interested in acquiring CBRN materials and threaten to use them."[35] Terrorists could readily detonate explosives placed next to radioactive material, and there is much fear about the consequences of an attack. Yet the probability of an RDD attack is unknown (see "Difficult Metrics"), terrorists would face impediments to launching a successful attack, and there has been no successful RDD attack as of May 2011. While the public tends to infer threat and probability from feasibility and fears, the reality is more complex.

---

[32] H. Rosoff and D. von Winterfeldt, "A Risk and Economic Analysis of Dirty Bomb Attacks on the Ports of Los Angeles and Long Beach," *Risk Analysis*, vol. 27, no. 3 (2007), pp. 533-546.

[33] JiYoung Park, "The Economic Impacts of Dirty Bomb Attacks on the Los Angeles and Long Beach Ports: Applying the Supply-Driven NIEMO (National Interstate Economic Model," *Journal of Homeland Security and Emergency Management*, vol. 5, no. 1 (2008), article 21, p. 10, http://www.bepress.com/jhsem/vol5/iss1/21/.

[34] Prepared statement of Kenneth Sheely, Associate Assistant Deputy Administrator for Global Threat Reduction, National Nuclear Security Administration, in House Homeland Security Committee, *Status Report on Federal and Local Efforts to Secure Radiological Sources*, p. 13. The study referenced is Los Alamos National Laboratory, *Economic Impacts of Detonating Radiological Dispersion Devices*, February 15, 2008, LA-CP-08-00973.

[35] James Clapper, Director of National Intelligence, "Statement for the Record on the Worldwide Threat Assessment of the U.S. Intelligence Community for the Senate Committee on Armed Services," March 10, 2011, p. 3, http://armed-services.senate.gov/statemnt/2011/03%20March/Clapper%2003-10-11.pdf.

It appears feasible for terrorists to acquire the radioactive material needed to build an RDD. Such material is in "widespread use in nearly every country,"[36] and there are questions about the vulnerability of facilities housing sealed sources to a carefully planned terrorist attack. Security of sources is discussed in detail in "Preventing an Attack."

Another aspect of the threat is that theft of one device could result in several RDDs. According to NNSA, "Some devices have more than one radioactive source, and a single source can be subdivided into smaller pieces to create more than one radiological dispersal device (RDD) or radiation exposure device (RED). If a theft were to occur responders should be prepared for the potential of multiple RDD/RED events."[37]

While the Nuclear Security Summit of April 2010 focused on protecting the world against terrorist use of nuclear weapons, some leaders expressed concern about RDDs. Pakistani Prime Minister Syed Yusuf Raza Gilani said, "We need strong national actions and greater international coordination to prevent illicit trafficking in nuclear materials. The threat of terrorist acts involving 'dirty bombs' is more real and it has global dimensions. We should take additional measures to combat this threat."[38] A news report stated, "Ahead of the [Nuclear Security Summit] conference, German Chancellor Angela Merkel made it clear that she, too, sees dirty bombs in terrorist hands as an even larger threat than regular nuclear weapons. Merkel said Monday that such weapons 'must not under any circumstances' fall into the hands of terror groups such as al Qaeda. 'We believe that the IAEA must be strengthened, we are ready to pledge additional finances to make this happen.'"[39] At a conference, "Global Efforts in WMD Threat Reduction," held at the Canadian Embassy in Washington on March 11, 2011, speakers representing several governments indicated that security of radiological sources would play a much more prominent role at the 2012 Nuclear Security Summit in Seoul than was the case at the 2010 summit. Cho Hyun, the sherpa for the Republic of Korea, suggested including the security of radioactive materials in the agenda of the 2012 summit.[40] (A "sherpa" is the individual in charge of a nation's preparations for a summit meeting.)

U.S. officials have expressed concern about RDDs but do not imply an immediate threat. Dennis Blair, then Director of National Intelligence, stated, "We judge that, if al-Qa'ida develops chemical, biological, radiological, or nuclear (CBRN) capabilities and has operatives trained to use them, it will do so. Counterterrorism actions have dealt a significant blow to al-Qa'ida's near-term efforts to develop a sophisticated CBRN attack capability, although we judge the group is still intent on its acquisition."[41] Robert Mueller III, Director of the Federal Bureau of

---

[36] U.S. Department of State. Office of the Coordinator for Counterterrorism. *Country Reports on Terrorism 2009*, August 2010, p. 200, http://www.state.gov/documents/organization/141114.pdf.

[37] U.S. Department of Energy. National Nuclear Security Administration. Global Threat Reduction Initiative. "GTRI Table Top Exercise Series Lessons Learned," March 2010, p. 3.

[38] Pakistan. Press Information Department. "Opening Remarks: Threat of Nuclear Terrorism," Prime Minister's Intervention at the Dinner Session on 12 April 2010, http://www.pid.gov.pk/ pm_Opening%20Dinner%20Remarks%20Final13410.doc.

[39] CBS News, "Obama Opens Summit with Optimism," April 12, 2010 (Monday), http://www.cbsnews.com/stories/ 2010/04/12/world/main6386991.shtml.

[40] Cho Hyun, Deputy Minister for Multilateral and Global Affairs, Ministry of Foreign Affairs and Trade, Republic of Korea, "Preparation for Nuclear Security Summit 2012 and Possible Deliverables," presentation at the Ninth ROK-UN Conference on Disarmament and Nonproliferation Issues, Jeju, Republic of Korea, December 3, 2010, available via http://jejuprocess.tistory.com/entry/Session-3-Enhancing-Nuclear-Security-and-Preventing-Nuclear-Terrorism.

[41] Dennis C. Blair, Director of National Intelligence, "Annual Threat Assessment of the US Intelligence Community for the Senate Select Committee on Intelligence," February 2, 2010, p. 9, http://www.dni.gov/testimonies/ 20100202_testimony.pdf.

Investigation, testified, "Al Qaeda remains committed to its goal of conducting attacks inside the United States ... al Qaeda's continued efforts to access chemical, biological, radiological, or nuclear material pose a serious threat to the United States."[42] According to a State Department report, "Some terrorists seek to acquire radioactive materials for use in a radiological dispersal device."[43]

Over the years, there have been thefts of radioactive material and attempts to use it for malevolent ends, and a few have been successful, as the following examples show:[44]

- (1993) "The Russian mafia allegedly places gamma ray-emitting pellets in the office of a Moscow businessman, resulting in the man's death."

- (1995) "Chechen rebels partially bury a container with a small quantity of cesium-137 in Moscow's Ismailovsky Park. The Chechen leader then notifies a Russian television crew, which locates the container."

- (1998) "19 small tubes of cesium are reported missing from a locked safe in a Greensboro, North Carolina hospital. ... The incident is deemed as a theft ... The cesium has not been recovered."

- (1998) "the Russian-backed Chechen Security Service announces the discovery and defusing of a container hidden near a railway line that was filled with radioactive materials and attached to an explosive mine. Chechen rebels involvement is suspected."

- (1999) "unidentified thieves attempt to steal a container housing 200g of radioactive material from a chemical factory in Grozny, Chechnya. One of the thieves dies half an hour after being exposed to the container. The other is hospitalized in critical condition. Each carried the container for only a few minutes."

- (2003) "evidence uncovered in Herat, Afghanistan, leads British intelligence agents and weapons experts to conclude that Al Qaeda has succeeded in constructing a small dirty bomb, though the device has not been found."

- (2003) "Thai police arrest a public school teacher in Bangkok after he attempts to sell a container filled with cesium-137 for $240,000."

- (2004) "British authorities arrest an alleged terrorist cell that was apparently plotting to create dirty bombs from the radioactive sources inside smoke detectors. (It would require millions of smoke detectors to collect enough radioactive material for a potent RDD.)"

- (2005) "Russian authorities report that they found documents in Chechnya on producing RDDs."

---

[42] Robert S. Mueller, III, Director, Federal Bureau of Investigation, "Statement Before the House Committee on Appropriations, Subcommittee on Commerce, Justice, Science, and Related Agencies," March 17, 2010, pp. 2-3, http://appropriations.house.gov/Witness_testimony/CJS/Robert_Mueller.3.17.10.pdf.
[43] U.S. Department of State. Office of the Coordinator for Counterterrorism. *Country Reports on Terrorism 2009,* August 2010, p. 200, http://www.state.gov/documents/organization/141114.pdf.
[44] These examples are from Nuclear Threat Initiative, *Radiological Terrorism Tutorial,* "History of Radiological Incidents," http://www.nti.org/h_learnmore/radtutorial/chapter03_01.html.

- (2006) "Alexander Litvinenko, a former Russian spy, was poisoned with radioactive polonium-210."

But fears and feasibility do not equate to threat, and murders, thefts, documents, a made-for-TV demonstration, "sting" operations, and foiled or poorly planned terrorist plots do not rise to the level of a successful RDD attack. The threat is plausible, but as with any high-consequence/low-frequency event, the sample size (at least using publicly-available information) is not large enough to support predictions of the likelihood of such an attack.

It would be much harder for terrorists to launch an *effective* RDD attack,[45] as distinct from making a crude RDD, for reasons such as the following. While no one of them presents an insurmountable obstacle, the combination may help explain why an attack of this sort has not occurred, and indeed could help deter attack by reducing the probability of success.

- Terrorists would need to know something about radiation. Various forms of radiation cause damage in differing ways. Alpha and beta emitters are most damaging inside the body, while gamma and neutron emitters are damaging inside or outside the body. Different radionuclides emit different amounts of energy when they decay, as **Figure 1** shows. Higher-energy radiation causes more biological damage. Even terrorists who were willing to die in an attack would need to know something about radiation safety for self-protection, as they could die if they did not handle the material properly, or if they did not know the curie content of material they had obtained.

- Terrorists would need to know something about radioactive materials. Obtaining the wrong material could render an RDD useless. Materials with very short half-lives (e.g., a week or less) would have to be used quickly and would produce negligible long-term contamination. Materials with very long half-lives (over 100,000 years) would be undesirable for an RDD because only an enormous mass, possibly tons, could generate enough radiation to pose a threat. Different radionuclides emit different amounts of energy when they decay, as **Figure 1** shows, and higher-energy radiation causes more biological damage. Chemical characteristics are also important. Some compounds dissolve in water more readily than others. Some elements (including their radioactive isotopes) and some chemical compounds bond more strongly to concrete and tile than others, making cleanup difficult.[46][47]

- Terrorists would have to conceal their actions, locations, and identities from law enforcement and intelligence services of many nations.

- Terrorists would have to obtain the material. NRC regulations enhance security for high-risk sources in the United States. While lost and abandoned sources exist, it would be hard to locate them in the United States or elsewhere. An attack

---

[45] In this report, "Value of RDDs for Terrorists" discusses potential effects of an attack, and "Impact of an Attack" discusses difficulties of finding a suitable metric for attack effectiveness.

[46] J. Real, F. Persin, and C. Camarasa-Claret, "Mechanisms of Desorption of 134Cs [cesium-134] and 85Sr [strontium-85] Aerosols Deposited on Urban Surfaces," *Journal of Environmental Radioactivity,* vol. 62, no. 1 (2002), pp. 1-15, http://www.ncbi nlm nih.gov/pubmed/12141602.

[47] Cesium is a constituent element of several chemical compounds (e.g., cesium chloride), as is strontium. Some of these compounds bond strongly to concrete, while others do not. Information provided by William Rhodes, Sandia National Laboratory, personal communication, December 17, 2010.

---

that aimed to seize radioactive materials might (or might not) meet armed resistance. It may be possible to obtain radioactive sources by using bogus means to obtain licenses, as GAO did,[48] but NRC has tightened guidelines for licensing to counter that risk. Other nations have different, and in some cases lower, standards for protecting radioactive material than does the United States, so it may be easier to obtain sources abroad, but they would have to be smuggled in, risking detection at multiple points along the way.

- Terrorists might want to extract the material from its capsule or other container, exposing them to radiation, possibly in lethal doses. This is particularly the case for Category 1 and 2 sources. If terrorists sought to create a bomb by placing an unopened sealed source next to explosives, it would be less effective.

- Terrorists would have to ensure the device dispersed material over the desired area. An RDD that dispersed material too widely might contaminate a large area to a very low level, while one that dispersed material over a very limited area, less than a city block, would place only that area off-limits, permitting workers to concentrate remediation efforts there. A wind shift could blow the material away from the target. A considerable amount of material might not disperse at all.

- Terrorists would have to move the material past detectors at U.S. ports of entry and at various places within the United States.

- Terrorists would have to acquire the other materials and equipment for a bomb, assemble the bomb, and place it. Law enforcement work might detect such steps.

- Emergency response, such as public alerts, evacuation or shelter-in-place instructions, and medical care, could reduce casualties and panic.

- Forensic analysis might reveal the perpetrator of the attack and the country from which the radioactive and other materials originated; the possibility of retaliation might make countries think twice before helping terrorists conduct an attack.

- Terrorists might judge that an RDD attack would lead swiftly to attacks on terrorist groups and to worldwide implementation of more stringent measures to counter all types of terrorist threats, closing future opportunities, so they might see the "costs" of an RDD attack as outweighing the "benefits."

Area Contaminated by an RDD Attack and Cost to Decontaminate

Press articles sometimes point to scenarios showing that an RDD could contaminate a large area and that cleanup would be costly. The reality is more complex: area and cost depend on the maximum acceptable dose and other assumptions chosen for a scenario. **Figure 2** and **Figure 3**, from a study by Defence Research and Development Canada and Battelle,[49] illustrate the point. **Figure 2** shows plumes from an RDD under the following assumptions. The RDD contains 1,000 curies of cesium-137; it is explosive-driven and detonated at BC Place Stadium in Vancouver,

---

[48] U.S. Government Accountability Office. *Nuclear Security: Actions Taken by NRC to Strengthen Its Licensing Process for Sealed Radioactive Sources Are Not Effective*, GAO-07-1038T, July 12, 2007, http://www.gao.gov/new.items/d071038t.pdf.

[49] Tom Cousins and Barbara Reichmuth, *Preliminary Analysis of the Economic Impact of Selected RDD Events in Canada*, Defence Research and Development Canada and Battelle, PNWD-SA-7845, c. 2007.

BC; wind speed is 3 meters per second (6.7 mph); and other weather conditions (temperature, rain, humidity, wind speed and direction at different altitudes, etc.) are not considered. Plumes show contamination at four dose levels: 15, 30, 100, and 500 millirem (mrem) per year.[50] As **Figure 3** shows, area deemed contaminated and costs inflicted by the attack depend on dose. The outermost plume, with a dose of 15 mrem per year, covers 99 square miles (256 square km) and associated costs of $80 billion, while the innermost plume, with a dose of 500 mrem per year covers 2.3 square miles (6 square km), with associated costs of $10 billion.

Figure 2. Area Contaminated by an RDD Attack

Using 1,000 Curies of Cesium-137

Source: Tom Cousins and Barbara Reichmuth, *Preliminary Analysis of the Economic Impact of Selected RDD Events in Canada*, Defence Research and Development Canada and Battelle, PNWD-SA-7845, c. 2007.

---

[50] Dose in the affected area would diminish continuously over time because of radioactive decay and weather effects (e.g., rain moving particles of material into the ground, providing some shielding). As a result, radioactive material that produced a given dose in the first year postattack would produce a progressively lower dose in each subsequent year. Cost figures are in Canadian dollars.

Figure 3. Area Contaminated to Various Levels, and Resulting Costs

For an Attack Using 1,000 Curies of Cesium-137

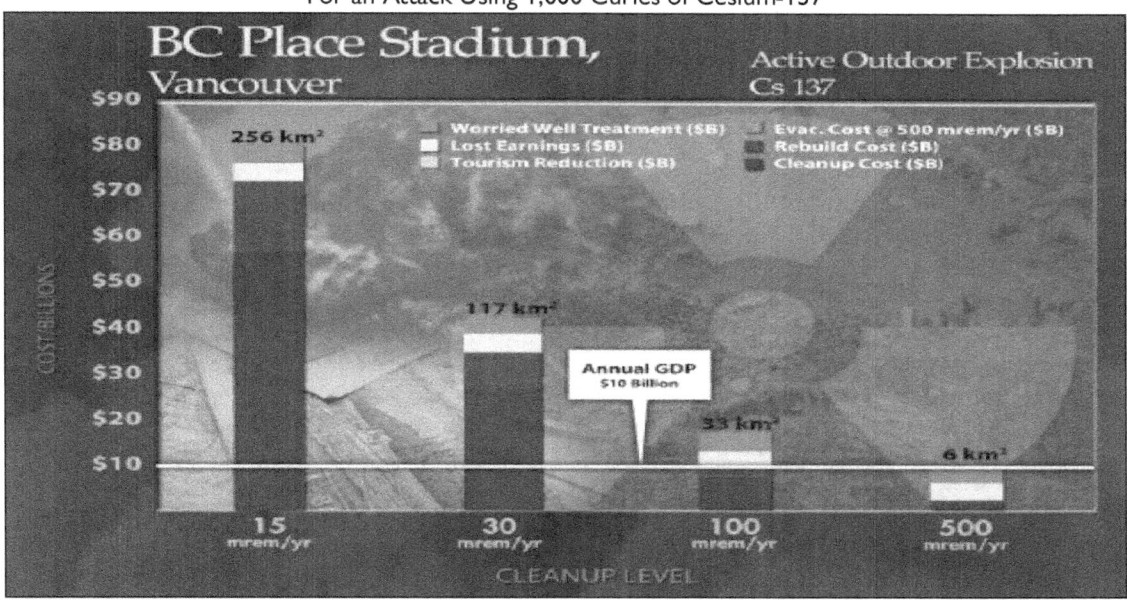

Source: Tom Cousins and Barbara Reichmuth, *Preliminary Analysis of the Economic Impact of Selected RDD Events in Canada*, Defence Research and Development Canada and Battelle, PNWD-SA-7845, c. 2007.

Preventing an Attack

The United States and other nations use a "layered defense" strategy in seeking to prevent an RDD attack. No layer is expected to be perfect, but each increases the likelihood of disrupting a terrorist attack. International, federal, state, and local organizations have added measures since 9/11 to prevent an RDD attack, and existing measures have been strengthened. (As discussed under "Attack Response, Recovery, and Attribution," programs to respond to an attack have also increased.)

Domestic Efforts

Before September 11, 2001, the main concern for radioactive sources was their safe handling. They were used worldwide in many applications with varying levels of security. While the United States undertook some security measures prior to the attacks, the ongoing U.S. response to the attacks includes new or augmented approaches to reducing the threat that radioactive sources may pose. One is to protect sources through licensing, tracking, and physical security upgrades. Another is to remove sources that are outside the tracking system because they are abandoned or lost ("orphan sources") or because they have been stolen for illegitimate uses, whether for an RDD or for scrap metal. A third is to reduce the number of sources in use. Different programs apply to one or more of these categories.

Securing Radioactive Sources

Since materials of greatest concern for use in an RDD are made in nuclear reactors, terrorists could only obtain them through transfer from sympathetic insiders, theft, or purchase. Securing radioactive sources therefore reduces the risk of an RDD attack. Many government agencies and other entities have taken steps to secure these sources; a few key examples follow.

Nuclear Regulatory Commission

NRC is an independent agency. It "has the responsibility to license and regulate the civilian use of radioactive materials for commercial, industrial, academic, and medical purposes in a manner that protects public health and safety and promotes the common defense and security. NRC and its predecessor, the Atomic Energy Commission (AEC), have regulated the use of radioactive materials since 1946."[51]

The Atomic Energy Act of 1954, P.L. 83-703, amended the Atomic Energy Act of 1946. The 1954 act, as amended, "is the fundamental U.S. law on both the civilian and the military uses of nuclear materials."[52] Section 161 gave the AEC the authority to regulate radioactive material "to promote the common defense and security or to protect health or to minimize danger to life or property." Section 11 of the act defined "special nuclear material" as uranium enriched in the isotopes 233 or 235, plutonium, and other material as specified by the AEC, and defined "byproduct material" as "any radioactive material (except special nuclear material) yielded in or made radioactive by exposure to the radiation incident to the process of producing or utilizing special nuclear material," and tailings or wastes from uranium or thorium ore. Byproduct material cannot be used as the active material in a nuclear weapon, but some types of it could be used in an RDD. Section 274 authorized NRC to enter into agreements with states (so-called "Agreement States"), giving them the authority to license and regulate byproduct and certain other radioactive material for public health and safety; NRC retained the authority to issue regulations for the common defense and security. As of March 31, 2011, 37 states had entered into such agreements, and NRC was evaluating additional states for participation in the program.[53]

Two other acts are particularly relevant to RDDs. The Energy Reorganization Act of 1974, P.L. 93-438, abolished the AEC and created the NRC. Section 201 transferred "all the licensing and related regulatory functions" of the AEC to NRC.[54] Section 651 of the Energy Policy Act of 2005, P.L. 109-58, defined "radiation source" as Category 1 or Category 2 sources as per the IAEA Code of Conduct and other material as determined by NRC, required NRC to issue regulations governing exports and imports of radiation sources, required NRC to establish a mandatory tracking system for radiation sources in the United States, and established a Task Force on

---

[51] U.S. Nuclear Regulatory Commission. "Request for Comments on the Draft Policy Statement on the Protection of Cesium-137 Chloride Sources and Notice of Public Meeting," NRC-2010-0209, *Federal Register,* vol. 75, no. 124, June 29, 2010, p. 37484.

[52] U.S. Nuclear Regulatory Commission. "Our Governing Legislation," http://www.nrc.gov/about-nrc/governing-laws.html.

[53] U.S. Nuclear Regulatory Commission. "Agreement State Program," http://www.nrc.gov/about-nrc/state-tribal/agreement-states.html.

[54] The Atomic Energy Act, as amended, and the Energy Reorganization Act, as amended, are available in U.S. Nuclear Regulatory Commission. Office of the General Counsel. *Nuclear Regulatory Legislation,* 107th Congress, 1st Session, NUREG-0980, vol. 1, no. 6, 2002, http://www.nrc.gov/reading-rm/doc-collections/nuregs/staff/sr0980/ml022200075-vol1.pdf#pagemode=bookmarks&page=14.

Radiation Source Protection and Security.[55] Section 652 required licensees to fingerprint any individual permitted unescorted access to certain radioactive material.

NRC has used these authorities to issue orders and regulations to enhance radiation source security since the 9/11 attacks. For example, it issued an order in 2005 to improve the security of irradiators having more than 10,000 curies,[56] a rule in 2005 on security policy for import and export of radioactive materials,[57] and an order in 2006 regarding fingerprinting and criminal history.[58] Also in 2005, it issued an "Order Imposing Increased Controls (Effective Immediately)" to licensees authorized to possess 16 types of radioactive material above certain "quantities of concern."[59] These quantities are the same as Category 2 sources in the IAEA Code of Conduct. The order required licensees to "allow only trustworthy and reliable individuals, approved in writing by the licensee, to have unescorted access to radioactive material quantities of concern and devices" and to "have a documented program to monitor and immediately detect, assess, and respond to unauthorized access," imposed requirements for transportation of radioactive materials, and required physical controls for mobile or portable devices containing radioactive material in quantities of concern.[60] The NRC website has a full listing of its security orders.[61] In the *Federal Register* of June 15, 2010, NRC published for comments a proposed rule, "Physical Protection of Byproduct Material," that would incorporate and modify some previous orders as 10 CFR 37.[62] The proposed rule would deal with "the security requirements for use of category 1 and category 2 quantities of radioactive material."[63]

Almost all of NRC's budget is for nuclear reactors—licensing, safety, fuel, and spent fuel management.[64] However, NRC has many programs for security of radioactive sources. It issues orders and regulations for licensees; inspects licensees to ensure compliance; and takes enforcement action as needed. In January 2009, it instituted the web-based National Source Tracking System to track Category 1 and 2 sources throughout their life cycle as required by the

---

[55] The Energy Policy Act is available at http://www.epa.gov/oust/fedlaws/publ_109-058.pdf.
[56] U.S. Nuclear Regulatory Commission, "In the Matter of All Panoramic and Underwater Irradiators Authorized to Possess Greater than 370 Terabecquerels (10,000 Curies) of Byproduct Material in the Form of Sealed Sources; Order Imposing Compensatory Measures (Effective Immediately)," *Federal Reguster,* vol. 68, no. 114, June 13, 2003, pp. 35458-35462. NRC redacted specific requirements except for those on handling information.
[57] U.S. Nuclear Regulatory Commission, "Export and Import of Radioactive Materials: Security Policies," final rule, *Federal Register,* vol. 70, no. 126, July 1, 2005, pp. 37985-37994.
[58] U.S. Nuclear Regulatory Commission. "In the Matter of Holders of Material Licenses Authorized to Manufacture or Distribute Items Containing Radioactive Materials of Concern; Order Imposing fingerprinting and Criminal History Records Check Requirements for Unescorted Access to Certain Radioactive Material and Modification of the Additional Security Measures (Effective Immediately)," *Federal Register* 71, October 27, 2006, pp. 63046-63050.
[59] U.S. Nuclear Regulatory Commission. "Order Imposing Increased Controls (Effective Immediately)," EA 05-090 in the matter of licensees authorized to possess radioactive material quantities of concern, November 14, 2005, http://adamswebsearch2 nrc.gov/idmws/doccontent.dll?library=PU_ADAMS^PBNTAD01&ID=053260115.
[60] U.S. Nuclear Regulatory Commission. "Increased Controls for Licensees That Possess Sources Containing Radioactive Material Quantities of Concern," Attachment B to "Order Imposing Increased Controls (Effective Immediately)," http://adamswebsearch2.nrc.gov/idmws/doccontent.dll?library=PU_ADAMS^PBNTAD01&ID=053260013.
[61] U.S. Nuclear Regulatory Commission. "Security Orders." http://www nrc.gov/reading-rm/doc-collections/enforcement/security/index html#6.
[62] U.S. Nuclear Regulatory Commission. "Physical Protection of Byproduct Material; Proposed Rule," *Federal Register,* vol. 75, no. 114, June 15, 2010, pp. 33902-33947.
[63] Ibid., p. 33904.
[64] U.S. Nuclear Regulatory Commission. *Congressional Budget Justification for FY 2011,* NUREG-1100, volume 26, February 2010, p. 3, http://www.nrc.gov/reading-rm/doc-collections/nuregs/staff/sr1100/v26/sr1100v26.pdf.

Energy Policy Act of 2005.[65] As of March 2010, this system tracked over 70,000 sources, of which 93 percent were cobalt-60, 3.5 percent were iridium-192, and 3 percent were cesium-137.[66] In response to a GAO investigation that used bogus means to obtain a license to procure radioactive material (see note 48), NRC changed licensing procedures to make them more secure. It is responding, or has responded, to other GAO criticisms.[67] It maintains a Nuclear Material Events Database to track incidents and accidents that involve nuclear material.[68] It operates the Agreement States program discussed earlier.

National Nuclear Security Administration

NNSA is a semiautonomous agency within the Department of Energy. One of NNSA's components is Defense Nuclear Nonproliferation (DNN). DNN's main program to enhance the security of radioactive sources is the Global Threat Reduction Initiative (GTRI). Most of GTRI's budget is for international programs, but it operates domestic programs as well, and the two are complementary in that they both help secure the United States and they draw on a common body of knowledge. The FY2012 budget request for Defense Nuclear Nonproliferation is $2,549.5 million, and for GTRI, $508.3 million.[69]

GTRI's Domestic Materials Protection Program provides security enhancements for domestic radioactive sources on a voluntary basis. NNSA funds the security upgrades at a facility and their initial maintenance, but the facility must agree to provide subsequent maintenance of the upgrades.[70] NRC and NNSA state that this program complements NRC's security program for these sources, with NRC setting the baseline for security and GTRI providing security upgrades at GTRI's expense for NRC licensees requesting assistance. Typically, a GTRI team visits a site to assess how security might be improved and negotiates contracts to have equipment installed. Equipment needs are site-specific; examples are iris scanners to control access, radiation detectors and TV cameras to monitor intrusion, equipment to link alarms to local police, and stronger doors and locks. NNSA has also developed In-Device Delay units that GTRI retrofits into irradiators that use cesium chloride as the active material in order to give police more time to respond to attempted thefts. **Figure 4** and **Figure 5** show security devices.

---

[65] For information on this system, see U.S. Nuclear Regulatory Commission. "National Source Tracking System," http://www.nrc.gov/security/byproduct/nsts html.

[66] U.S. Nuclear Regulatory Commission. National Source Tracking System: Blog. "Fun Facts about NSTS!," entry of March 12, 2010, http://www nrc.gov/security/byproduct/nsts/blog html.

[67] U.S. Nuclear Regulatory Commission. "Summary of NRC Actions [in] Response to GAO Reports," March 19, 2010, http://www.nrc.gov/reading-rm/doc-collections/congress-docs/correspondence/2010/carper-03-19-2010.pdf.

[68] U.S. Nuclear Regulatory Commission. "Nuclear Material Events Database," http://nmed.inl.gov/.

[69] U.S. Department of Energy. Office of Chief Financial Officer. *FY 2012 Congressional Budget Request,* volume 1, National Nuclear Security Administration. February 2011, DOE/CF-0057, p. 325, http://www.cfo.doe.gov/budget/12budget/Content/Volume1.pdf.

[70] U.S. Department of Energy. National Nuclear Security Administration. "NNSA: Securing Domestic Radioactive Material," fact sheet, February 1, 2011, p. 2, http://nnsa.energy.gov/print/mediaroom/factsheets/domestic.

Figure 4. Iris Reader

Source: Photo by CRS

Notes: This biometric device is in use to control access to a room with radioactive material. It was installed through a contract with Global Threat Reduction Initiative. The user looks into the two brown ovals, and the device scans the irises to determine if the person is authorized for access.

Figure 5. Radiation Detector

Source: Black Cat Systems

Notes: Radiation detectors alarm when radiation is released. (This model is an example only, and is not necessarily used to comply with NRC regulations.)

Many sources in the United States, mostly low-level, have been lost, abandoned, or stolen; are excess to a user's needs; or have become significantly less radioactive through decay. Another part of GTRI's work, therefore, is recovering radioactive sources. The Off-site Source Recovery Project (OSRP), another GTRI program, performs this task. As of March 28, 2011, OSRP had recovered 24,029 sources in the United States totaling 801,560 curies;[71] while many were small and many were well protected, some were "orphan" sources that were lost or abandoned. NNSA expects to remove at least 2,200 excess sources within the United States each year.[72]

GTRI also operates a course, Alarm Response Training, at the Y-12 National Security Complex for local law enforcement officers. As described by Kenneth Sheely, Associate Assistant Deputy Administrator for GTRI, "Most on-site guards at facilities with radioactive sources are not armed or large enough force strength to neutralize the threat. Therefore, the key responders are often off-site local law enforcement. Unfortunately, many local law enforcement officials are not made aware of the nature of the material which is in use at hospitals, blood banks, universities, oil fields, and manufacturing plants in their jurisdiction. It is important for their safety, and the safety of their communities, that they receive proper training about radiological sources."[73] The course involves classroom instruction on what radioactive materials might be encountered; the threat this

---

[71] Los Alamos National Laboratory, "OSRP Sources Recovered," as of March 28, 2011, http://osrp.lanl.gov/images/ Maps/Recoveries_to_Date.pdf.

[72] U.S. Department of Energy. Office of Chief Financial Officer. *FY 2011 Congressional Budget Request.* volume 1, National Nuclear Security Administration, DOE/CF-0047, February 2010, p. 439, http://www.cfo.doe.gov/budget/ 11budget/Content/Volume%201.pdf.

[73] "Prepared Statement of Kenneth Sheely," Associate Assistant Deputy Administrator for Global Threat Reduction, National Nuclear Security Administration, in U.S. Congress. House Homeland Security Committee, *Status Report on Federal and Local Efforts to Secure Radiological Sources,* p. 17.

material poses; how to use detection equipment; and operational exercise scenarios. GTRI, the NNSA Office of the Under Secretary for Counterterrorism, and the FBI also provide table top exercises to provide a site-specific scenario for organizations holding NRC licenses for radioactive material and for managers at all levels of government to exercise their response to a terrorist attack.[74]

GTRI programs within the United States operate on a small scale compared to their universe of potential coverage. As of February 2011, GTRI had done the following.[75] It had identified more than 2,700 buildings in the United States with high-priority radiological materials, and had completed security upgrades at 251 of them, "with the remainder aiming to be completed by 2025." It had provided its Alarm Response Training course to 1,118 local law enforcement officers. It had installed delay devices on 238 irradiators. GTRI's pace has picked up since late summer 2009. At that time, GTRI had completed security upgrades for 37 of about 2,200 buildings, provided its Alarm Response Training course to 175 personnel, and installed delay devices on 32 irradiators.[76] However, much work remains, some of which is presented in **Appendix B**.

Relationship Between NRC and NNSA Programs

NRC and NNSA view their programs as complementary. According to a joint statement by the two agencies, NRC and Agreement States (see "Nuclear Regulatory Commission") have created "a strong and effective regulatory framework that includes licensing, inspection, and enforcement" that "provides a *common baseline level of security to ensure adequate protection* of public health and safety and the common defense and security." NNSA works with NRC and others "to *build on the existing regulatory requirements by providing voluntary security enhancements.*"[77] A radiation safety officer who has partnered with GTRI expressed a similar view.[78] (Radiation safety officers, as discussed later, are in charge of the safety and security of radioactive materials at their facilities.)

> NRC and GTRI have the same goal—no RDD attacks—but different roles. NRC has the regulatory role. Licensees must follow its rules, which must be prescriptive enough to improve security for all licensees that have quantities of concern; yet flexible enough to cover large panoramic irradiators, research universities, and hospital blood banks. NRC must enforce its rules impartially. When it interacts with a licensee, it cannot be too sensitive to that licensee's situation because anything they do for one could affect how they treat others. In contrast, GTRI is not a regulator. It has a mandate to spend its funds to make partner sites more secure. It is a voluntary program, and can be responsive to local site conditions. For example, it may suggest security enhancements at a site, and the licensee may accept some, reject some that wouldn't work there, and modify others. If the outcome improves security, GTRI will work with the site.

---

[74] Ibid., p. 17.

[75] U.S. Department of Energy. National Nuclear Security Administration. "NNSA: Securing Domestic Radioactive Material," fact sheet, February 1, 2011, p. 2.

[76] "Prepared Statement of Kenneth Sheely," pp. 16-17.

[77] U.S. Nuclear Regulatory Commission and National Nuclear Security Administration., "Partnership for Securing Nuclear and Radioactive Materials," enclosure to U.S. Nuclear Regulatory Commission, "Development of a Joint NRC-NNSA Key Messages Document, 'Partnership for Securing Nuclear and Radioactive Materials,' (FSME-10-029)," March 31, 2010, http://www.nrc.gov/reading-rm/doc-collections/for-the-record/2010/protection-02-01-10.pdf. Emphasis in original.

[78] Personal communications, August and September 2010.

This complementary relationship might lead some to ask whether the NRC and GTRI programs should be combined to eliminate some overlap. The radiation safety officer just quoted, however, argued against doing so:

> These different roles set up tensions between GTRI and NRC. GTRI has a lot of freedom because it is not the regulator, but it must work hard to keep the "blessing" of the NRC and agreement states because licensees will not work with GTRI if NRC or agreement states tell them not to. At the same time, GTRI wants to keep NRC out of their process. Having NRC or agreement state staff accompany GTRI to the sites would change GTRI's relationship with licensees. I would not have partnered with GTRI if NRC was part of the process because during GTRI's security evaluation of our site, we had the freedom to identify weaknesses. Licensees won't show their problems to NRC for fear of being cited. As the regulator, NRC cannot give assurances that violations uncovered during a voluntary site visit will not be cited. So, I think GTRI shouldn't be partnering with NRC.

Radiation Source Protection and Security Task Force

The Energy Policy Act of 2005 established the task force with a mandate to "evaluate, and provide recommendations relating to, the security of radiation sources in the United States from potential terrorist threats, including acts of sabotage, theft, or use of a radiation source in a radiological dispersal device." Its members represent 12 federal agencies and another four invited agencies or organizations, with the NRC chairman or a designee as the chair.[79] It is charged with reporting every four years; it released its most recent report in August 2010.[80] It "identified two major challenges that require attention at higher levels." First, access to disposal pathways for unused sources, "already a challenge before 2006, has diminished substantially since that time, and a comprehensive policy change is needed to overcome current barriers in the disposal framework."[81] It recommended initiating or continuing efforts to develop, evaluate, and investigate options for disposal of sources. Second, the task force examined alternatives to several risk-significant radioactive sources. It pointed to three alternative technologies for existing sources: using the same radionuclide but in a different form, replacing one radionuclide with another, and using a technology (e.g., x-rays) in place of radioactive material. The report focused on cesium-137 chloride, which "has long received increased attention from both a safety and security perspective because of its potential dispersibility if removed from an irradiator or source capsule."[82] The report recommended increased support to develop alternative technologies, investigation of options to replace Category 1 and 2 sources, and review of whether licensing for Category 1 and 2 cesium-137 chloride sources should be discontinued.[83]

---

[79] Members of the task force are the Chairman of the NRC, Secretary of Homeland Security, Secretary of Defense, Secretary of Energy, Secretary of Transportation, Attorney General, Secretary of State, Director of National Intelligence, Director of the Central Intelligence Agency, Administrator of Federal Emergency Management Agency, Director of Federal Bureau of Investigation, and Administrator of Environmental Protection Agency. Other invited agencies are Department of Health and Human Services, Office of Science and Technology Policy, Organization of Agreement States (non-voting member), and Conference of Radiation Control Program Directors (non-voting member).

[80] U.S. Radiation Source Protection and Security Task Force. *The 2010 Radiation Source Protection and Security Task Force Report,* August 2010, http://www.nrc.gov/security/byproduct/2010-task-force-report.pdf.

[81] Ibid., p. 32.

[82] U.S. Radiation Source Protection and Security Task Force. *The 2010 Radiation Source Protection and Security Task Force Report,* p. 40.

[83] Ibid., p. 45.

Other Agencies

Other agencies have responsibilities for security as well. For example, the Environmental Protection Agency (EPA) "is seeking to reduce the number of sealed radiation sources used in industrial devices and applications. Through its Alternative Technologies Initiative, the Agency has been working with industry since 2001 to identify non-nuclear substitutes."[84] This program seeks to reduce the risk of industrial and environmental contamination and to protect sources from seizure by terrorists. The Domestic Nuclear Detection Office is supporting R&D for the same purpose through its Small Business Innovative Research program. The Department of Defense (DOD) has some sealed sources in the United States, such as at hospitals. In such instances, NRC grants DOD components, such as the Army, one or more licenses, and they protect the sources in accordance with NRC regulations.[85]

How Secure Are Radioactive Sources in the United States?

An RDD attack is possible but its probability is unknowable. On the one hand, the NRC notes common violations of security procedures, including "failure to escort all unauthorized individuals" with access to Category 1 and 2 sources, "inoperable or ineffective physical protection systems," "incomplete or inadequate plan with local law enforcement," "ineffective barriers that can be easily defeated or bypassed," and "failure to restrict access to only individuals with a need to know and who have been determined trustworthy and reliable."[86] The NRC reported that in FY2010, no Category 1 or 2 sources were lost; three Category 3 sources were lost and recovered; and a Category 3 source fell into the Gulf of Mexico from an oil platform and was not recovered.[87] The FY2010 Radiation Source Protection and Security Task Force report stated, "Every year, thousands of sources become disused and unwanted in the United States. While secure storage is a temporary measure, the longer sources remain disused or unwanted the chances increase that they will become unsecured or abandoned."[88] Most of these sources have a very low level of radioactivity and do not pose a significant risk.[89] Security of radioactive sources has been upgraded since 9/11, but enhanced security measures, such as those of GTRI, have not been completed. **Appendix B** discusses some of the tasks that GTRI has completed and those that remain.

On the other hand, there have been "no successful thefts or sabotage" of Category 1 or 2 sources,[90] and there has never been a successful RDD attack. The NRC's Nuclear Material Events Database shows that from the third quarter of FY2006 through the second quarter of FY2010, no Category 1 sources were lost, and 17 Category 2 sources were lost but all were recovered.[91] For

---

[84] U.S. Environmental Protection Agency. "Alternative Technologies for Industrial Applications," http://www.epa.gov/radiation/source-reduction-management/alt-technologies.html.

[85] Information provided by Chemical, Biological, Radiological, and Nuclear Directorate, Office of Homeland Defense Integration and Defense Support of Civil Authorities, Office of the Secretary of Defense, Department of Defense, personal communication, September 15, 2010, and by Nuclear Regulatory Commission, February 10, 2011.

[86] U.S. Nuclear Regulatory Commission. "Security Inspections and Enforcement," briefing slides 5-8, no date. NRC provided these slides to CRS July 31, 2010.

[87] U.S. Nuclear Regulatory Commission. *Nuclear Material Events Database: Annual Report, Fiscal Year 2010*, http://nmed.inl.gov/AnnualReports/NMEDFY10%20Annual.pdf, p. ix.

[88] U.S. Radiation Source Protection and Security Task Force. *The 2010 Radiation Source Protection and Security Task Force Report*, p. 31.

[89] Personal communication, Nuclear Regulatory Commission, November 30, 2010.

[90] U.S. Nuclear Regulatory Commission. "Security Inspections and Enforcement," slide 19.

[91] Idaho National Laboratory, "Nuclear Material Events Database: Quarterly Report, Second Quarter Fiscal Year (continued...)

---

the period 1994 to 2005, the 2006 report of the Radiation Source Protection and Security Task Force found

> an average of about 5 lost or stolen risk-significant sources per year. In approximately 80 percent of the events for the 12-year period, the sources were recovered. This results in an average of about one unrecovered source per year. Ninety-five percent of these lost and stolen sources were Ir-192 [iridium-192] sources in radiography cameras that were lost/stolen primarily because of the licensee's failure to meet requirements. Because of the short half-life of Ir-192 (74 days), these sources quickly decayed, and the current risk posed by these sources is negligible."[92]

It is unclear if this record is due to security measures, terrorist ineptness or disinterest, other factors, or some combination.

Views from the Field

Many types of radioactive sources, including those in Categories 1 and 2, require NRC licenses. The license is issued to a company, university, or other organization. The person responsible for ensuring that the licensee maintains the safety and security of these sources is the radiation safety officer (RSO). Since RSOs are the front line of radioactive source security in the United States, they are in a position to provide "ground truth." Accordingly, CRS conducted eleven interviews with RSOs, ten by telephone and one in writing. Four RSOs were at industrial facilities, one was at a hospital complex, and six were at universities. Seven had worked or were working with GTRI; four had not done so. This section draws on these interviews, which also provide the basis for some issues and options for Congress, discussed later. CRS has withheld names, locations, and some other details to avoid compromising facility security.

RSOs are generally trained in safety, not security; many have advanced degrees in health physics or similar fields. Prior to 9/11, security was a very small part of their work. They learned about security through their work, often partnering with human resources (HR) personnel, local or university law enforcement, lawyers, and security consultants. Based on CRS analysis, security entails a different set of skills and a different culture. A central presumption of a safety culture is that everyone is operating in good faith. No one wants to be a victim of a radiological accident, and everyone recognizes that they must follow certain procedures to protect themselves and others. A safety culture involves protecting people, e.g., through shielding and simple access controls like door locks to prevent accidental exposure. In contrast, a central presumption of a security culture is that terrorists, who may include insiders, may attempt to steal a radioactive source in order to make an RDD and would look for security vulnerabilities. A security culture therefore involves protecting radioactive sources through more robust means.

Before 9/11, RSOs focused on safety. Security sometimes consisted of a standard door lock on a room with radioactive sources, mainly to prevent inadvertent exposure; security served safety. All RSOs noted that security, and security awareness, at their facilities has improved since 9/11: "Sometimes it seems that sources are so secure that I can't get to them." One said, "The sources

---

(...continued)

2010," by Thomas Smith and Robert Sant, INL/EXT-10-18136 (FY 2010 Qtr 2), July 2010, p, 5. Annual reports of the database are available at http://nmed.inl.gov/.

[92] Radiation Source Protection and Security Task Force, report, 2006, section "Recovery of Lost or Stolen Sources." A 74-day half-life results in the decay of about 99.9% of the material in 2 years (approximately ten half-lives).

are more secure in the sense that there is now a defined program with security as its main purpose," but raised an issue of how security is defined: "It is unclear whether the sources themselves are 'more secure' since there were no instances where subversive terrorist activity was uncovered as a result of the [NRC] security program enhancements and no evidence that there was a credible threat of theft or sabotage prior to the security enhancements." RSOs attributed much of the credit for increased security to orders from NRC. The Increased Controls (IC) order of 2005 laid out the framework for actions required to boost security. Among other things, this order required licensees to limit unescorted access to Category 1 and 2 sources to people the licensee deemed trustworthy and reliable (T&R); monitor those sources, detect unauthorized access, and respond promptly to such access; and have a pre-arranged response plan with local law enforcement. An order of 2003 for panoramic irradiators of more than 10,000 curies directed licensees to take specific security measures (that were not made public), and an order of 2006 required licensees to have the FBI fingerprint and review the criminal history record of people to be granted unescorted access to Category 1 and 2 sources.[93]

Most RSOs said that the IC order made a great difference. It set out in general terms what needed to be done, and gave RSOs a "very clear justification," as one said, for requesting funds for security upgrades. In response to the order, facilities installed security equipment, which varied from site to site. Examples include the use of cameras and radiation detectors linked to a security station to monitor rooms with radioactive materials, and use of key cards and stronger doors and door locks to control access.

In another response to the IC order, RSOs worked with police officers to ensure an armed response to a theft of a radioactive source. Police departments at several universities had sworn officers who were armed. Most RSOs felt that the police could provide an armed response to an alarm within a few minutes. In practice, though, one said, the response would depend on what else the police were responding to at the time. Response time seemed less certain for small facilities located away from major cities. RSOs said that the police understand the significance of a radioactive source stolen by terrorists; some RSOs provided training on that topic, and in other cases police took a course at the Y-12 National Security Complex (TN) offered by GTRI.

RSOs expressed divergent views on T&R investigations. Some saw the T&R requirement as "a giant pain in the neck." In this view, it is difficult to vet applicants, very few if any are rejected, checks of personal references are of no value because the applicant provides the references, the process takes an "inordinate" amount of time, and NRC guidance is unclear. Others saw the requirement as quite manageable. At several facilities, RSOs organized a process for vetting applicants, hired contractors to obtain the needed data, and had personnel who were skilled at personnel evaluations decide if an applicant was T&R, and convened a committee meeting to examine cases where T&R might be denied. One RSO said that the cost for each T&R investigation was minimal, such as $100 for a local criminal history check and $32 for an FBI background check. NRC has considered extending security measures for Class 1 and 2 sources to Class 3 sources as well, though the idea has not gained traction. An RSO expressed concern that if NRC extended T&R requirements to Category 3 sources, which are far more numerous than Category 1 and 2 sources, the process would become extremely burdensome.

Each institution developed its own criteria for T&R. This was typically done in cooperation with the organization's HR office and, in the case of universities, with the university police

---

[93] For references to these orders, see "Nuclear Regulatory Commission," above.

department. Criteria vary from one institution to another, but may include academic record; a police and FBI background investigation and fingerprint check; personal references; and credit, residence, and employment history. A few mounted a significant effort to define criteria. Several said they had criteria but needed the flexibility to weight the significance of events in people's lives when deciding on T&R. Several said their T&R process looked for a pattern of behavior rather than specific criteria. RSOs did not share their T&R criteria with RSOs from other organizations because they saw the criteria as proprietary. As a result, an individual might be declared T&R by one organization but not by another.

Some foreign graduate students and postdoctoral fellows seek T&R for unescorted access to use equipment needed for their research. RSOs found it difficult to gather the requisite data. Typically, students have college transcripts but not an employment history. It is difficult to gather financial data, and if the student provided personal references, it is hard to judge their credibility. Some information may be provided in foreign languages, adding another layer of difficulty. Nonetheless, some universities were able to grant foreign nationals unescorted access; another denied all foreign nationals unescorted access.

CRS inquired about the balance between prescriptiveness and flexibility of NRC orders. That is, should orders prescribe uniform standards for source security, such as installing specific devices, or should orders be performance-based, stating the desired outcome but leaving it to individual facilities to select the means best suited to achieving that outcome? NRC opted for the latter in the IC order. Some RSOs expressed frustration at the lack of clarity over what was needed to meet that order. Should they buy certain equipment, and how much was too much or not enough? Others felt that a performance-based approach provided flexibility. They noted that security measures needed may vary even from room to room, such as whether a heavy irradiator is on the first or fourth floor of a building. Requiring the same measures in all cases would, in this view, lead to unnecessary expenses and would make it easier for terrorists to figure out what security systems they would have to overcome at any facility. Another RSO said, "Performance-based requirements are the only way that this program can be implemented in any reasonable manner." Since there are significant design differences even among facilities designed for the same purpose, specifying a particular practice "would not necessarily be universally applicable."

One way in which NRC could be prescriptive is to mandate that facilities be secure against a "design basis threat" (DBT), which specifies in detail the type of threat that a facility must be able to repel; a hypothetical example would be an attack by six terrorists armed with rocket-propelled grenades and AK-47s, perhaps aided by insiders. NRC requires nuclear power plant operators to be able to protect against a DBT to ensure adequate security. Several RSOs saw a DBT as unnecessary and burdensome, requiring an "over-the-top" response. One who had dealt with DBTs in another job felt that they produced "a multitude of scenarios" that led to "pretty bizarre stuff." Another felt that a DBT might be useful for guidance, but a high enough threat could force facilities to close because it would become too costly to meet the threat.

Several RSOs were most concerned about an insider threat. An insider might kill others at the facility, sabotage the facility, or help outsiders gain access to it. An insider familiar with the security systems might be able to defeat them. CRS observes that T&R screening would not necessarily foil this threat because T&R applies only to people needing unescorted access to Category 1 and 2 sources, a category that often excludes most people at a facility.

RSOs who had worked with GTRI had high praise for the program: "They've been great." "GTRI did a fantastic job." "The program evaluations that they have done meshed perfectly with the philosophy of the US NRC security requirements and provided a much needed independent review and assessment of the facility program." GTRI staff came to their facilities, provided a security assessment, recommended a security plan, worked out with the RSOs and others (e.g., campus police) which security devices to install, and contracted with contractors to install the devices. RSOs felt that GTRI staff were knowledgeable and professional. Examples of equipment installed include: in-device delay mechanism to increase the time it would take for terrorists to open an irradiator and steal its contents, thus providing more time for an armed response; iris scanners, a biometric device to control access; cameras to monitor devices with radioactive material; an infrared lighting system so people at central alarm stations could monitor radioactive devices if the lights go out; a system to provide backup power if power goes out; and links from alarms to police. Most felt that it was beneficial to have an outside group evaluate their security situation. One said that without the program his facility would not be upgrading security and pointed to a side benefit he expected from the upgrade, which was then in progress: A robust security system of the sort GTRI will install will send a message to people using the facility that security is important and they must follow guidance, helping instill a security culture. On the other hand, one RSO felt that some of the security measures seemed excessive, while another said that the added measures went a step beyond the real threat.

Detecting Radioactive Sources

U.S. Customs and Border Protection, a component of the Department of Homeland Security (DHS), has deployed systems at ports and border crossings to detect and identify radioactive material entering the United States. (Customs and Border Protection also screens people and goods entering the United States for guns, drugs, and other contraband.) In addition, other DHS components, notably the Coast Guard, Transportation Security Administration, and Office of Border Protection, deploy radiation detection equipment at other sites inside the United States, and the Domestic Nuclear Detection Office has a cooperative program with state and local agencies to deploy such equipment.

Deployed systems seek to detect terrorist nuclear weapons or nuclear-weapon material while minimizing the impact on legitimate commerce, but are of use for interdicting some potential RDD material as well. They are of two main types, passive radiation detection systems and radiography systems. (Radiography systems send a beam of x-rays or gamma rays through a cargo container or other item to be inspected to create a radiograph, an image similar to a medical x-ray.) As noted earlier, some types of RDD-usable materials are strong gamma-ray emitters. In contrast, nuclear weapon materials (certain isotopes of uranium and plutonium) give off fewer gamma rays that are, on average, much less energetic. As a result, currently-deployed radiation detectors, such as radiation portal monitors,[94] could easily detect RDD-usable material if unshielded. Therefore, such material would in all likelihood be shielded, and even a tiny amount would require heavy shielding. A thick enough layer of lead would stop enough gamma rays to preclude detection by radiation detectors, but a thicker shield is more likely to be visible as an area of dense matter on a radiograph.

Efforts are underway at national laboratories, universities, and corporations in the United States and other nations to improve existing detection technologies and to develop new ones based on

---

[94] See U.S. Department of Homeland Security. Customs and Border Protection. "Radiation and Portal Monitors Safeguard America from Nuclear Devices and Radiological Materials," no date, accessed July 15, 2010, http://www.cbp.gov/xp/cgov/border_security/port_activities/cargo_exam/rad_portal1.xml.

different physical principles. The science of detection and nine detection technologies are discussed in detail in CRS Report R40154, *Detection of Nuclear Weapons and Materials: Science, Technologies, Observations*, by Jonathan Medalia.

Since detection systems offer a high probability of detecting RDD-usable material within their range, terrorists intent on an RDD attack would try to evade detection. Very little shielding would render small alpha and beta sources undetectable. It would be difficult for technical means to detect radioactive material smuggled across unguarded stretches of the U.S. border; interdiction in that scenario would depend on border security. Terrorists could avoid detection equipment at ports of entry by obtaining radioactive material within the United States. Radiation detectors are deployed along some major highways and choke points (e.g., bridges) within the United States; terrorists could transport RDD material along routes without detectors if they knew where detectors were located. The United States takes technical and other measures in response. A struggle between offense and defense, or between hiders and seekers, is a common military and homeland-security issue.

Intelligence and Counterterrorism

To thwart terrorist attacks using CBRN weapons, intelligence must be collected, analyzed, and acted upon. This section notes some U.S. government agencies involved in this effort and what they do. A more detailed description is beyond the scope of this report, and descriptions of RDD-specific intelligence and counterterrorism efforts would involve classified information. It is also beyond the scope of this report to delve into shortcomings or improvements in intelligence collection, analysis, and sharing, or in the ability to act on intelligence. Several CRS reports provide additional information.[95]

Many U.S. government agencies contribute and analyze intelligence on potential CBRN terrorist threats. However, in its analysis of intelligence and other failures preceding the 9/11 attacks, the 9/11 Commission noted shortcomings in the Intelligence Community and recommended unity of effort "across the Foreign-Domestic Divide," "in the Intelligence Community," "in Sharing Information," and "in the Congress."[96] In response, Congress passed the Intelligence Reform and Terrorism Prevention Act of 2004 (IRTPA, P.L. 108-458). This act established the position of Director of National Intelligence (DNI), who is to "serve as head of the intelligence community" and "act as the principal adviser to the President, to the National Security Council, and the Homeland Security Council for intelligence matters related to the national security."[97] Section 6905, "Radiological Dispersal Devices," makes it unlawful to acquire or possess RDDs.

Some agencies focus on intelligence outside the United States. IRTPA established the National Counterterrorism Center (NCTC, Section 1021) and directed the President to establish the National Counter Proliferation Center (NCPC, Section 1022). According to IRTPA, the NCTC is

---

[95]See CRS Report R41022, *The National Counterterrorism Center (NCTC)—Responsibilities and Potential Congressional Concerns* , by Richard A. Best Jr. CRS Report RL33539, *Intelligence Issues for Congress*, by Richard A. Best Jr.; CRS Report RL34231, *Director of National Intelligence Statutory Authorities: Status and Proposals*, by Richard A. Best Jr. and Alfred Cumming; and CRS Report R41004, *International Terrorism and Transnational Crime: Security Threats, U.S. Policy, and Considerations for Congress*, by John Rollins and Liana Sun Wyler

[96] National Commission on Terrorist Attacks upon the United States, *The 9/11 Commission Report*, New York, Norton, 2004, p. vii.

[97] For further information, see U.S. Office of the Director of National Intelligence, "ODNI Fact Sheet," October 2010, http://www.dni.gov/content/ODNI%20Fact%20Sheet_Oct2010.pdf.

"to serve as the primary organization in the United States Government for analyzing and integrating all intelligence possessed or acquired by the United States Government pertaining to terrorism and counterterrorism, excepting intelligence pertaining exclusively to domestic terrorists and domestic counterterrorism." It is "to conduct strategic operational planning for counterterrorism activities, integrating all instruments of national power, including diplomatic, financial, military, intelligence, homeland security, and law enforcement activities within and among agencies," though the NCTC director "may not direct the execution of counterterrorism operations." It is also "to serve as the central and shared knowledge bank on known and suspected terrorists and international terror groups."[98] The NCPC is to be "a primary organization within the United States Government for analyzing and integrating all intelligence possessed or acquired by the United States pertaining to proliferation."[99]

Within the United States, the Federal Bureau of Investigation (FBI) is the lead agency for counterterrorism intelligence. This authority derives from several sources. The U.S. Code (Title 18, Section 2332b(f)), gives the Attorney General "primary investigative responsibility for all Federal crimes of terrorism." The Code of Federal Regulations states that the FBI Director "shall … [e]xercise Lead Agency responsibility in investigating all crimes for which it has primary or concurrent jurisdiction and which involve terrorist activities or acts in preparation of terrorist activities within the statutory jurisdiction of the United States. Within the United States, this would include the collection, coordination, analysis, management and dissemination of intelligence and criminal information as appropriate."[100] Homeland Security Presidential Directive 5 states, "Generally acting through the Federal Bureau of Investigation, the Attorney General, in cooperation with other Federal departments and agencies engaged in activities to protect our national security, shall also coordinate the activities of the other members of the law enforcement community to detect, prevent, preempt, and disrupt terrorist attacks against the United States."[101] A congressional report observes, "the FBI created a Directorate of Intelligence in its headquarters to produce intelligence analysis and to provide an institutional home for its analysts. In an effort to create this so-called 'agency within an agency,' the FBI created a National Security Branch at its headquarters composed of its Counterterrorism and Counterintelligence Divisions and the new Directorate of Intelligence."[102]

Global Efforts

Securing Radioactive Sources

Because an RDD attack might occur outside the United States, or material obtained abroad might be used for an RDD attack on this nation, international organizations, the United States,

---

[98] For further information on NCTC, see its website at http://www.nctc.gov.

[99] For further information on NCPC, see its website at http://www.counterwmd.gov/index.htm.

[100] Code of Federal Regulations, Title 28 (Judicial Administration), Chapter 1 (Department of Justice), Part 0 (Organization of the Department of Justice), subpart p-1 (Office of Justice Programs and Related Agencies), 0.85 (general functions), (l), http://cfr.vlex.com/vid/0-85-general-functions-19677030.

[101] Homeland Security Presidential Directive 5, Management of Domestic Incidents, is available at http://www.dhs.gov/xabout/laws/gc_1214592333605.shtm#1.

[102] "A Ticking Time Bomb: Counterterrorism Lessons from the U.S. Government's Failure to Prevent the Fort Hood Attack," a special report by Joseph I. Lieberman, Chairman, and Susan M. Collins, Ranking Member, United States Senate Committee on Homeland Security and Governmental Affairs, February 3, 2011, p. 53, http://hsgac.senate.gov/public/_files/Fort_Hood/FortHoodReport.pdf.

nongovernmental organizations, and others have taken steps to secure sources worldwide.[103] Some are discussed here.

International Organizations

International Atomic Energy Agency (IAEA): The IAEA, one of the United Nations family of organizations, has responsibilities in such areas as nuclear energy, peaceful applications of nuclear science and technology, nuclear nonproliferation, and nuclear safety and security. It has the lead international role in efforts to secure radioactive sources. It has taken many types of actions toward this goal, such as the following:

- In March 2001, its Board of Governors approved a Code of Conduct on the Safety and Security of Radioactive Sources. In light of the 9/11 attacks, the IAEA issued a revised Code of Conduct in 2003.[104] As of January 2011, 101 nations had made a political commitment regarding the code.[105]

- In 2002, the board approved a Plan of Activities to Protect Against Nuclear Terrorism.[106] In 2003, the agency held an International Conference on Security of Radioactive Sources.[107] In 2005, the Board of Governors approved a Nuclear Security Plan for 2006-2009 focusing on protecting nuclear and other radioactive material, detection of and response to malicious acts involving such material, and information coordination and analysis.[108] The 2010-2013 Nuclear Security Plan covers four areas: "Needs Assessment, Information Collation and Analysis"; "Contributing to the Enhancement of a Global Nuclear Security Framework"; "Providing Nuclear Security Services"; and "Risk Reduction and Security Improvement."[109] The plan defines nuclear security as "The prevention and detection of and response to theft, sabotage, unauthorized access, illegal transfer or other malicious acts involving nuclear material, other radioactive substances or their associated facilities."[110] As of March 2010, the agency had begun implementing the 2010-2013 plan.[111]

---

[103] This section excludes U.N. Security Council Resolution 1540 (2004) because it addresses proliferation of nuclear, chemical, and biological weapons and their means of delivery, but not radiological weapons.

[104] International Atomic Energy Agency, "Code of Conduct on the Safety and Security of Radioactive Sources," 2004, http://www-pub.iaea.org/MTCD/publications/PDF/code-2004_web.pdf.

[105] International Atomic Energy Agency, *List of States that have a made a political commitment with regard to the Code of Conduct on the Safety and Security of Radioactive Sources and the Supplementary Guidance on the Import and Export of Radioactive Sources*, January 21, 2011, http://www.iaea.org/Publications/Documents/Treaties/codeconduct_status.pdf.

[106] International Atomic Energy Agency, "Nuclear Security," http://www-ns.iaea.org/security/default htm.

[107] See http://www.iaea.org/worldatom/Press/Focus/RadSources/index.shtml.

[108] International Atomic Energy Agency, "Nuclear Security."

[109] International Atomic Energy Agency. Board of Governors. General Conference. "Nuclear Security Plan 2010-2013." GOV/2009/54-GC(53)/18, August 17, 2009, pp. 8-12, http://www-ns.iaea.org/downloads/security/nuclear-security-plan2010-2013.pdf.

[110] Ibid., p. 1.

[111] Yukia Amano, Director General, International Atomic Energy Agency, "Introductory Statement to Board of Governors," March 1, 2010, http://www.iaea.org/NewsCenter/Statements/2010/amsp2010n001.html#security.

- In March 2003, the agency organized an International Conference on Security of Radioactive Sources. The conference, which was held in Vienna, had participants and observers from 123 countries.[112]

- The agency provides technical assistance to countries in locating and removing orphan radioactive sources. In July 2006, for example, it helped Georgia's Ministry of Environment find and recover two such sources. The agency states, "The technical assistance provided by the IAEA to Georgia is part of its global effort to improve the security of radioactive sources and nuclear material."[113] Other elements of this assistance include training courses in Asia, Africa, and South America "to help guide the development of national strategies for regaining control over sealed sources," and training for customs authorities in radiation monitoring.[114]

- The agency maintains an International Catalogue of Sealed Radioactive Sources and Devices, providing detailed information to help identify sealed sources so they can be handled safely.[115]

- The agency maintains an Illicit Trafficking Database, which tracks incidents involving nuclear and other radioactive materials; as of September 2010, 111 states participated in it.[116]

G8 Global Partnership: In June 2002, the G8 committed itself to "six principles to prevent terrorists or those that harbour them from acquiring or developing" CBRN weapons, established the G8 Global Partnership Against the Spread of Weapons and Materials of Mass Destruction to implement these principles, and committed to raise "up to $20 billion" over ten years for projects supporting the Global Partnership.[117] Since then, the Global Partnership has launched many programs to reduce CBRN threats. For example, according to a 2010 G8 report, "The recovery of several hundred highly radioactive Radioisotopic Thermoelectric Generators (RTGs) from the Northern Sea Route, the Baltic Sea, and the Russian Far East has made significant progress and continues with support from Canada, Finland, France, Norway, and the United States." Further, "The United States and Russia are partnering to place equipment for radiation detection at border crossings to detect and prevent the illicit cross-border trafficking of nuclear and radiological materials."[118] However, the 2010 G8 summit in Canada did not commit to providing added funds to continue the work of the Global Partnership, leaving its fate beyond 2012 uncertain. Instead, the final declaration noted the global economic situation and stated,

---

[112] International Atomic Energy Agency, *Security of Radioactive Sources,* proceedings of an international conference held in Vienna, Austria, 10-13 March 2003 ..., 2003, http://www-pub.iaea.org/MTCD/publications/PDF/Pub1165_web.pdf.

[113] International Atomic Energy Agency. "Radioactive Sources Recovered in Georgia," July 27, 2006, http://www.iaea.org/newscenter/news/2006/georgia_radsources.html.

[114] International Atomic Energy Agency, "Improving the Safety and Security of Sealed Radioactive Sources," accessed May 2, 2011, http://www.iaea.org/Publications/Booklets/SealedRadioactiveSources/activities.html.

[115] International Atomic Energy Agency, "International Catalogue of Sealed Radioactive Sources and Devices (ICSRS)," http://nucleus.iaea.org/CIR/CIR/ICSRS.html, updated 2010.

[116] International Atomic Energy Agency, "Illicit Trafficking Database (ITDB)," accessed April 26, 2011, http://www-ns.iaea.org/security/itdb.asp.

[117] G8, "The G8 Global Partnership Against the Spread of Weapons and Materials of Mass Destruction," June 27, 2002, http://www.g7.utoronto.ca/summit/2002kananaskis/arms.html.

[118] G8, "Report on the G-8 Global Partnership 2010," last modified February 11, 2011, http://www.canadainternational.gc.ca/g8/summit-sommet/2010/muskoka-globalpartnership-muskoka.aspx?lang=eng.

> We recognize the continuing global threats before us, and we all recognize the importance of continuing our joint efforts as partners to address them in the years ahead. Toward that end, we ask our senior experts to evaluate the results of the Global Partnership to date, as a point of departure for developing options for programming and financing beyond 2012, focusing on nuclear and radiological security, bio security, scientist engagement ...[119]

There were also questions about whether all G8 members contributed their pledged amounts.[120]

Global Initiative to Combat Nuclear Terrorism: This initiative was established in 2006 by 13 governments.[121] Its principles include "Develop, if necessary, and improve accounting, control and physical protection systems for nuclear and other radioactive materials and substances," and "Improve the ability to detect nuclear and other radioactive materials and substances in order to prevent illicit trafficking in such materials and substances, to include cooperation in the research and development of national detection capabilities that would be interoperable."[122] As of September 2010, it had 82 partner nations.[123]

U.S. Programs

National Nuclear Security Administration: NNSA's Office of Defense Nuclear Nonproliferation has programs addressing radiological material overseas.[124] GTRI has international as well as domestic programs. It seeks "to identify, secure, remove and/or facilitate the disposition of high risk vulnerable nuclear and radiological materials around the world, as quickly as possible, that pose a threat to the United States and the international community."[125] GTRI includes programs for international radiological material removal and international nuclear and radiological material protection. The Off-site Source Recovery Project, discussed above, focuses on sources within the United States, but has also removed 985 sources from 15 other nations as of September 2010.[126] Another NNSA program, Second Line of Defense (SLD), "strengthens the capability of foreign governments to deter, detect, and interdict illicit trafficking in nuclear and other radioactive materials across international borders and through the global maritime shipping system."[127] Megaports, part of SLD, deploys radiation detection equipment at seaports; NNSA plans to complete installations at four ports in FY2011, for a total of 45.[128] The SLD Core program "plans to install radiation detection equipment at an additional 55 foreign sites

---

[119] G8, *G8 Muskoka Declaration: Recovery and New Beginnings*, Muskoka, Canada, June 25-26, 2010, p. 9, http://g8.gc.ca/wp-content/uploads/2010/07/declaration_eng.pdf.

[120] Chris Schneidmiller, "G-8 Nonproliferation Program Faces Uncertain Future," *Global Security Newswire*, August 16, 2010.

[121] For links to key documents on the Global Initiative, see U.S. Department of State. "The Global Initiative To Combat Nuclear Terrorism," http://www.state.gov/t/isn/c18406 htm.

[122] U.S. Department of State. Bureau of International Security and Nonproliferation. "Statement of Principles." http://www.state.gov/t/isn/rls/other/126995 htm.

[123] U.S. Department of State. Bureau of International Security and Nonproliferation. "Partner Nation List," 2010, http://www.state.gov/t/isn/c37083.htm; and personal communication, Department of State, September 22, 2010.

[124] Descriptions of these programs are accessible through Department of Energy, National Nuclear Security Administration, "Nuclear Nonproliferation," http://www nnsa.energy.gov/nuclear_nonproliferation/index htm.

[125] U.S. Department of Energy. National Nuclear Security Administration. "GTRI: Reducing Nuclear Threats," January 2009, http://www nnsa.energy.gov/news/2330.htm.

[126] Los Alamos National Laboratory, Off-site Source Recovery Program, "OSRP Operations Worldwide."

[127] Department of Energy, *FY 2011 Congressional Budget Request*. volume 1, p. 371.

[128] Ibid., p. 380. For more detail on Megaports, see U.S. Department of Energy. National Nuclear Security Administration. "Megaports Initiative." October 2009, http://nnsa.energy.gov/nuclear_nonproliferation/documents/SLD-MegaportsBrochure-blue_v4-singles.pdf.

---

in Azerbaijan, Estonia, Georgia, Kazakhstan, Lithuania, Latvia, Romania, Bulgaria, Hungary, Russia, Ukraine, Kyrgyzstan, Poland, Mongolia, Turkey, Croatia, Pakistan, Tajikistan and Mexico, increasing the total non-Megaport sites with completed installations to 418."[129]

Nuclear Regulatory Commission: While NRC's role is mainly domestic, it has several international programs. It helps regulators in some other nations implement the IAEA Code of Conduct, such as by helping them develop and maintain national registries of radioactive sources, helping them with safety and security regulatory oversight, and holding workshops that describe NRC's requirements for physical protection of materials and the U.S. regulatory framework.[130] In FY2009, NRC "worked with the international community to implement consistent export and import guidance for civilian uses of radioactive materials, and ... provided regulatory assistance for the control of radioactive sources."[131]

Department of State: Several State Department programs work to reduce radiological threats. The Export Control and Related Border Security (EXBS) program strengthens border security and control of strategic exports, thereby "bolster[ing] partner countries' capabilities to detect and interdict illicit transfers of strategic items, radioactive materials, and other WMD components ... EXBS focuses on capacity building through legislation development, licensing and regulatory workshops, enforcement training, [and] provision of inspection and detection equipment ..." It assists 46 countries.[132] The department's Weapons of Mass Destruction Terrorism program conducts projects to counter a terrorist CBRN attack. The department also supports the Global Initiative to Combat Nuclear Terrorism, described above.

Department of Defense: Within the Department of Defense, the commander of the U.S. Strategic Command (USSTRATCOM) is "the lead combatant commander for integrating and synchronizing global WMD efforts."[133] The Defense Threat Reduction Agency (DTRA) "is the U.S. Department of Defense's official Combat Support Agency for countering weapons of mass destruction. Our people are Subject Matter Experts on WMD, and we address the entire spectrum of chemical, biological, radiological, nuclear and high yield explosive threats." [134] The U.S. Strategic Command Center for Combating Weapons of Mass Destruction is operated jointly by USSTRATCOM and DTRA. It "synchronizes Combating Weapons of Mass Destruction efforts across our military's geographic commands."[135]

---

[129] U.S. Department of Energy, *FY2011 Congressional Budget Request,* volume 1, p. 379.

[130] U.S. Nuclear Regulatory Commission and National Nuclear Security Administration, *Partnership for Securing Nuclear and Radiological Materials*, March 31, 2010, p. 2, http://www.doh.state.fl.us/environment/radiation/radmat/NRC-Items/sp10029.pdf.

[131] Nuclear Regulatory Commission, Office of International Programs, *NRC International Activities, Annual Report FY 2009*, October 2009, p. 2, http://www nrc.gov/about-nrc/ip/oip-annual-report-fy2009.pdf.

[132] U.S. Department of State., *Fiscal Year 2011 Congressional Budget Justification: Volume 2, Foreign Operations*, 2010, p. 176, http://www.state.gov/documents/organization/137936.pdf.

[133] U.S. Strategic Command. "USSTRATCOM Center for Combating Weapons of Mass Destruction (SCC-WMD)," February 2011, http://www.stratcom mil/factsheets/USSTRATCOM_Center_for_combating_Weapons_of_Mass_Destruction/.

[134] U.S. Department of Defense. Defense Threat Reduction Agency and USSTRATCOM Center for Combating WMD. "About DTRA/SCC-WMD," http://www.dtra mil/About.aspx.

[135] Ibid.

Programs of Other Nations

The United States, international organizations, and non-governmental organizations are not the only entities trying to secure radioactive material. Individual nations control their own material and contribute to efforts to secure such material elsewhere through legislation, waste repositories, exercises, source registries and tracking systems, contributions of funds or technical expertise, and the like. Efforts by Canada, Pakistan, Poland, and the Republic of Korea, described in this section, provide examples. This section draws on personal communications with embassy officials and on official documents; such material, of course, is positive in its outlook. An evaluation of the effectiveness of measures described here, however, is beyond the scope of this report.

Canada: Canada's Department of Foreign Affairs and International Trade provided the following information:

> In cooperation with DOE Global Threat Reduction Initiative (GTRI), Canada funded the removal of 59 radioisotopic thermoelectric generators (RTGs) along the Northern Sea route in the Russian Arctic and the Far East from 2007 to 2011, including disassembly and replacement by solar panels. Canada also provided funding for the manufacture of transportation and shielding containers for safe and secure relocation of RTGs, the removal of five RTGs in cooperation with Norway, and the development of a master plan for international donors to support the decommissioning, removal, and disposal of RTGs.[136]

Pakistan: In the past decade, Pakistan has augmented institutions to implement a safety and security regime for nuclear weapons and nuclear and radiological materials.[137] According to its website, the Pakistan Nuclear Regulatory Authority (PNRA) has as its mission "to ensure safe operation of nuclear facilities and to protect radiation workers, general public and the environment from the harmful effects of radiation by formulating and implementing effective regulations and building a relationship of trust with the licensees and maintain transparency in its actions and decisions."[138] PNRA is implementing a National Nuclear Security Action Plan (NSAP) in coordination with the IAEA. This plan manages high-risk radioactive sources, provides detection equipment at key points, secures orphan sources, etc. Pakistan is also cooperating with the IAEA to upgrade physical security for high-activity radioactive sources at a dozen medical centers. PNRA has licensed Pakistan's four blood irradiators, which "conform to the required safety and security standards as per IAEA recommendations and guidelines." PNRA's Nuclear Security Training Center offers courses in prevention, detection, and response to personnel from various national organizations. Pakistan has improved the capabilities of three nuclear security inspectorates and has established three more inspectorates that are charged with enhancing physical security of radioactive sources. The country has a Nuclear Security Emergency Coordination Center (NuSECC) to coordinate and support efforts of other government agencies in case of a nuclear or radiological incident.

Poland: Poland's Central Laboratory for Radiological Protection, created in 1957, is tasked with protecting the general population and persons in radiological occupations against ionizing

---

[136] Personal communication, May 24, 2011.

[137] Except as noted, material in this paragraph was provided by the Pakistani Embassy in Washington, DC, on May 17, 2011. See also Kenneth Luongo and Nasem Salik, "Building Confidence in Pakistan's Nuclear Security," *Arms Control Today,* December 2007, pp. 11-17.

[138] Pakistan Nuclear Regulatory Authority home page, http://www.pnra.org/.

---

radiation. Its duties include monitoring food and the environment for radioactive contamination, providing radiological emergency assistance, supporting countermeasures against trafficking in radioactive and nuclear materials, and conducting research and training.[139] Poland's state-owned Radioactive Waste Management Plant (RWMP) collects and solidifies low- and medium-activity radioactive waste produced in Poland, and prepares it for disposal in the National Radioactive Waste Repository. The latter, a near-surface repository operated by RWMP, began operations in 1961.[140]

Poland has taken several steps to secure radioactive material. It held an exercise in September 2004 that dealt with response to illicit trafficking of nuclear and radioactive material.[141] [142] Another exercise, organized in September 2010 by Poland's Interior Ministry and the U.S. Embassy in Warsaw, involved an RDD with cesium-137 in front of a soccer stadium. This exercise is related to the European soccer championship to be held in 2012; in connection with that event, Poland has appointed a Governmental Body against Chemical, Biological, Radiological and Nuclear Threat. Since 2004, the RWMP has been involved in the GTRI program for securing radioactive sources in Poland. That initiative has upgraded security systems in more than 70 institutions, including almost all oncology clinics and regional blood banks.

Republic of Korea: ROK has sought to secure radioactive material through managing radioactive waste, licensing material, and tagging mobile sources, among other things. Its Atomic Energy Act dates to 1958, and has been amended numerous times. Other laws deal with nuclear and radioactive material as well. Based on a 2008 Act on the Management of Radioactive Wastes, "on 2 January 2009, the Korean Radioactive Waste Management Corporation was established as an independent government agency for the safe and more efficient management of radioactive waste generated in Korea. It will be in charge of the construction and operation of a disposal facility for low-level and intermediate-level radioactive waste, the management of spent nuclear fuel and research-related activities."[143]

The Minister of Education, Science and Technology (MEST) is responsible for nuclear safety and regulation. Use, distribution, or manufacture of sources with higher dose rates or radioactivity requires a license from MEST.[144] The number of licenses has apparently increased over the years. According to the Korean Institute for Nuclear Safety (KINS), an autonomous agency reporting to MEST, "The number of institutions that use radioisotopes and radiation generators is on the

---

[139] Poland, Central Laboratory for Radiological Protection, http://www.clor.waw.pl/clor/clor_eng.htm.

[140] Poland, National Atomic Energy Agency, "National Report of Poland on Compliance with the Obligations of the Joint Convention on the Safety of Spent Fuel Management and on the Safety of Radioactive Waste Management," Polish 3rd National Report as Referred to in Article 32 of the Joint Convention, October 2008, p. 1, http://www.paa.gov.pl/en/doc/3rdreport_JointConv.pdf.

[141] G. Smagala, "Polish Efforts in the Fight Against Illicit Trafficking in Radioactive Sources," in International Atomic Energy Agency, *Safety and Security of Radioactive Sources: Towards a Global System for the Continuous Control of sources Throughout Their Life Cycle,* Proceedings of an International Conference, Bordeaux, 27 June-1 July 2005, pp. 166-168.

[142] Information in the balance of this paragraph was provided to CRS by the National Atomic Energy Agency, Warsaw, Poland, May 16, 2011.

[143] Organisation for Economic Co-operation and Development, *Nuclear Legislation in OECD Countries: Regulatory and Institutional Framework for Nuclear Activities: Korea,* 2009, p. 10, http://www.oecd-nea.org/law/legislation/korea.pdf.

[144] Republic of Korea, Korea Institute of Nuclear Safety, "Country Report on (RAS/9/042), 'Sustainability of Regional Radiation Protection Infrastructure,'" 2009, p. 17. This report was submitted to an IAEA Regional Cooperation Center by KINS; personal communication, Embassy of the Republic of Korea, Washington, DC, May 16, 2011.

---

increase from 70 in 1974 to about 3800 at the end of 2008."[145] ROK has a national register of radiation sources. KINS has developed a Radiation Safety Information System for "trac[ing] radiation sources from manufacture (or import) to disposal and to manage the inventory of radiation sources efficiently."[146] One of its components is the Life Cycle Management System for Radioisotopes and Radiation Generators. "In order to find out industrial radiography sources when they are stolen or misplaced, KINS has operated a real-time tracking system, START, under the support of the Korean government from 2006. ... Every [mobile terminal], attached on each industrial radiograph source, transfers its status data to the central control system established in KINS, and it monitors the location of the sources across the nation." In 2008, it monitored about 1,000 mobile sources used for industrial radiography.[147]

Non-Governmental Organizations

Partnership for Global Security: PGS, a nongovernmental organization, was founded as the Russian American Nuclear Security Advisory Council in 1997. It originally focused on cooperative threat reduction measures in the former Soviet states, but has broadened its scope to encourage cooperative efforts to reduce the CBRN threat globally. In the area of radiological weapons, for example, Kenneth Luongo, the president of PGS, wrote that the 2012 Nuclear Security Summit in Seoul "could endorse several actions in this area, beginning with an international commitment to secure all high-intensity radiological sources in public buildings with an immediate focus on major metropolitan hospitals. ... The summit could also endorse the establishment of regional radiological zones of security, where the countries in the region work together to ensure the security of radiological sources."[148]

World Institute for Nuclear Security: WINS, a nongovernmental organization, began operation in September 2008. Its goal is to provide a forum for nuclear security personnel worldwide to share best practices for security of nuclear and radiological material. Its focus is exclusively on security; in contrast, some organizations, like IAEA, focus on security and safety, and others, such as the World Association of Nuclear Operators, focus exclusively on safety. WINS publishes guides to best security practices, holds workshops, and provides security information to its members.[149]

How Secure Are Radioactive Sources in Other Nations?

Illicit Trafficking

The IAEA's Illicit Trafficking Database (ITDB) is a key source of information on the vulnerability of nuclear and other radioactive sources. As of June 2010, 110 nations reported data for this database to the IAEA. According to the agency,

---

[145] Ibid.

[146] Ibid., p. 22.

[147] Ibid.

[148] Kenneth Luongo, "The Urgent Need for a Seoul Declaration: A Road Map for the 2012 Nuclear Security Summit and Beyond," *Arms Control Today*, April 2011, p. 14.

[149] World Institute for Nuclear Security, *WINS Fact Sheet*, April 2010, http://www.wins.org/content.aspx?id=80.

16. From 1 July 2009 to 30 June 2010, States reported 222 incidents to the ITDB; 120 of these were reported to have occurred during this period and the remaining 102 were reports of prior incidents. Twenty-one of the incidents reported involved such activities as unauthorized possession and/or attempts to sell or smuggle nuclear material or radioactive sources. Sixty-one additional incidents involved the theft or loss of nuclear or other radioactive material; in 58% of those incidents, the material has not been reported as recovered.

17. One-hundred and forty reported incidents involved unauthorized activities without apparent relation to criminal activity. These included the detection of nuclear material or radioactive sources disposed of in unauthorized ways, the detection of radioactively contaminated material, the recovery of orphan sources and the discovery of nuclear material or radioactive sources in unauthorized or undeclared storage.[150]

According to the U.S. Department of State, "Of the 222 events reported to the IAEA from 1 July 2009 to 30 June 2010 involving radiological and nuclear materials outside legitimate control, most involved incidents overseas and roughly 10 percent occurred in the U.S. All of the incidents the U.S. reported to the IAEA during this time involved detections of radioactively contaminated materials coming into the U.S."[151]

The IAEA provided additional data and analysis.[152] In 2009, drawing on the ITDB, it reported "a persistent problem with illicit trafficking in nuclear and other radioactive materials, with thefts, losses and other unauthorized activities and events." Of the 1,562 confirmed incidents in the database for 1995-2008, 421 involved reports of theft or loss, which IAEA called "indicative of vulnerabilities in security and control systems." It noted that lost or stolen material had not been recovered in about 65 percent of the cases. Another 336 incidents involved unauthorized possession or related criminal activities. The report implied that the number could be higher: "Amateurish character and poor organization have been the characteristics of many trafficking cases; well-organized, professional and demand-driven trafficking would be much more difficult to detect." The 724 incidents of other unauthorized activities and events "have mainly involved radioactive sources, including some Category 1, 2, and 3 high-risk 'dangerous' sources, and radioactively contaminated materials. Occurrence of such incidents is an indication of failures in systems to control, secure and dispose of radioactive materials. They also show weaknesses of regulatory systems."

Examples

In some cases, described below, radioactive sources in other nations have been protected poorly or not at all. Poor protection gives rise to concern about the vulnerability of radioactive materials to acquisition by terrorists.

India: This nation has many small shops that buy scrap metal and process it for resale. In 2010, a shop in Mayapuri purchased a cobalt-60 irradiator and broke it apart, exposing workers to gamma radiation. The irradiator had been imported from Canada in 1968 and had been in storage at Delhi

---

[150] International Atomic Energy Agency, Board of Governors, *Nuclear Security Report 2010: Measures to Protect Against Nuclear Terrorism*, Report by the Director General, GOV/2010/42-GC(54)/9, August 12, 2010, p. 4, http://www.iaea.org/About/Policy/GC/GC54/GC54Documents/English/gc54-9_en.pdf.

[151] Personal communication, Department of State, May 6, 2011.

[152] Material on ITDB in this paragraph is from International Atomic Energy Agency, "IAEA Illicit Trafficking Database (ITDB)," September 2009, pp. 1-5, http://www-ns.iaea.org/downloads/security/itdb-fact-sheet-2009.pdf.

University since about 1985. A press report noted, "When the [chemistry] department decided to auction old machinery, Mr. [Deepak] Pental [vice chancellor of the university] said a committee of professors overseeing the process included the gamma irradiator because they assumed it had outlived its radioactive life." The incident killed one person and left six hospitalized.[153]

Thailand: In 2000, a disused cobalt-60 source was stored outdoors. Two scrap collectors bought it and took it to a junkyard where workers cut it open. Some workers had burn-like injuries. Not until 17 days after the source was first dismantled did medical authorities report a suspected radiation accident. Three people died, another seven had radiation injuries, and about 1,870 people living near the junkyard were exposed to radiation.[154]

Spain: In 1998, a steel factory in Los Barrios, Spain, melted a cesium-137 source. Vapors contaminated dust in the factory's filters. The dust was processed, ultimately contaminating 500 tons of material. Elevated levels of cesium-137 were soon detected in southern France and northern Italy. Six people had slight contamination as a result, but "the economic, political and social consequences were major. The estimated total costs for clean up, waste storage, and interruption of business at the affected companies exceeded $25 million US dollars."[155]

Egypt: In 2000, an iridium-192 source of 50 to 81 curies was being used to inspect welds on natural gas pipelines in Met Halfa. The source was not recovered after the job. A farmer found it and took it home. The farmer and his son died, and the rest of the family was hospitalized.[156]

Georgia: The Republic of Georgia is on a key smuggling route between Russia and the Middle East. Alexander Kupatadze, a postdoctoral fellow at George Washington University, wrote in 2010, "since 2002 thirteen criminal cases overall have been brought against smugglers of radioactive materials ... there were several cases in which ordinary people found radioactive sources on former Soviet military bases and sold them as scrap metal without knowing what they had ... in 2008, two former high-ranking police officers were caught trying to sell radioactive materials. According to investigators, an employee had stolen some cesium from the Mtskheta nuclear reactor, which serves as a storage facility for found orphan radioactive sources, and was collaborating with the former policemen to sell the cesium as uranium."[157]

Twenty-eight nations in Africa: In FY2009, NRC staff "participated in the first meeting of the 28-nation Forum of Nuclear Regulatory Bodies in Africa. ... [The members] expressed interest in NRC's ongoing or planned radioactive source-related assistance efforts, especially assistance to develop national registries of radioactive sources."[158] Such a registry, which would contain type, location, and other information for all risk-significant radioactive sources (IAEA Code of

---

[153] Jim Yardley, "Indian University Is Deemed Source of Radiation Exposure," *New York Times*, April 29, 2010.

[154] International Atomic Energy Agency, *Reducing Risks in the Scrap Metal Industry: Sealed Radioactive Sources*, Vienna, Austria, September 2005, p. 6, http://www.iaea.org/Publications/Booklets/SealedRadioactiveSources/pdfs/handout_scrap.pdf.

[155] Ibid, p. 5.

[156] Ahmed Hasan and Karim El-Adham, "Integrated Management Program for Radioactive Sealed Sources in Egypt (IMPRSS)," Presentation to ANES/SENA 2004 Symposium, Miami Beach, FL, October 3-6, 2004, http://www.osti.gov/bridge/purl.cover.jsp;jsessionid=B156C5D10CC6C9C1257795DB4DEE5072?purl=/840066-N41PeP/native/.

[157] Alexander Kupatadze, "Organized Crime and the Trafficking of Radiological Materials: The Case of Georgia," *Nonproliferation Review*, July 2010, pp. 222, 223, 228, http://cns miis.edu/npr/pdfs/npr_17-2_kupatadze.pdf.

[158] Nuclear Regulatory Commission, Office of International Programs, *NRC International Activities, Annual Report FY 2009*, October 2009, p. 11, http://www.nrc.gov/about-nrc/ip/oip-annual-report-fy2009.pdf.

Conduct Category 1 and 2 sources), is essential for regulating their safety and security; at a minimum, a nation cannot have confidence that owners of sources unknown to it are following required procedures.[159]

The foregoing information is troubling not only because it demonstrates poor security of radioactive sources (and consequent vulnerability to theft), but also because it shows security resting on a shaky foundation. **Figure 6**, based on CRS analysis, shows the relationship of steps to security and the chronological sequence, from bottom to top, in which they occur. At the top of the figure, security measures must be implemented, such as through regulation, deployment of security equipment, and means to track sources. Such measures cannot be implemented unless authorities recognize the need to secure sources. (Safety measures like simple door locks to protect people from inadvertent exposure to radioactive sources cannot be considered security measures because they would not hinder a terrorist group intent on stealing such sources.) But that recognition cannot occur unless authorities have recognized the need for radiation safety and implemented measures to that end. RDDs pose a threat to public safety, but if authorities do not see sources as a safety concern, they will have no reason to treat them as a security concern. Thus there can be a safety culture without a security culture but not the other way around. In the United States, for example, security measures were added on top of existing safety measures. In turn, recognizing the need for radiation safety requires understanding the hazards of radiation, which requires an understanding of radiation itself. Failure to implement adequate security measures implies a failure at other levels of the "pyramid" as well. Such an environment would facilitate terrorist acquisition of material for an RDD. ("Views from the Field" discusses differences between a safety culture and a security culture.)

Figure 6. Foundations of Radioactive Source Security

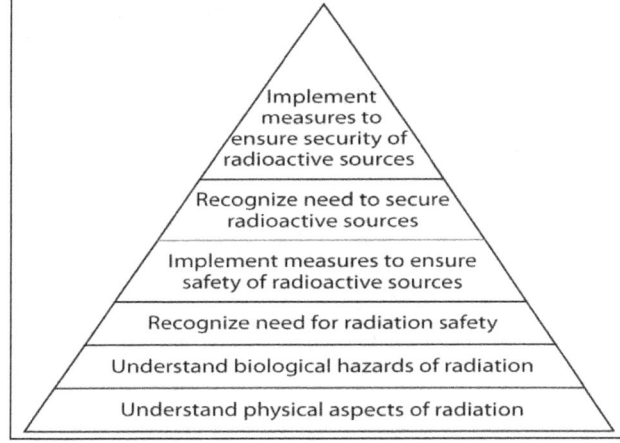

Source: CRS

---

[159] Personal communication, U.S. Nuclear Regulatory Commission, April 26, 2011.

Attack Response, Recovery, and Attribution

Organization and Planning for Response

If an attack occurred despite efforts at prevention, effective response could save lives, mitigate damage, and speed recovery. Accordingly, the federal government has devoted extensive resources to planning for a response. Key authorities for response are as follows.

- The Stafford Act authorizes the President to declare an event to be a disaster, thereby allowing federal agencies to assist state and local governments. According to FEMA, the "Robert T. Stafford Disaster Relief and Emergency Assistance Act, P.L. 100-707, signed into law November 23, 1988; amended the Disaster Relief Act of 1974, P.L. 93-288. This Act constitutes the statutory authority for most Federal disaster response activities especially as they pertain to FEMA and FEMA programs."[160]

- The Homeland Security Act of 2002 (P.L. 107-295) establishes the Department of Homeland Security. The department's missions include preventing terrorist attacks in the United States, reducing U.S. vulnerability to terrorism, minimizing damage from terrorist attacks, and aiding recovery from such attacks. The act establishes a Directorate of Emergency Preparedness and Response. The DHS Secretary, acting through the Under Secretary of Emergency Preparedness and Response, is responsible for "helping to ensure the effectiveness of emergency response providers to terrorist attacks, major disasters, and other emergencies" (section 502), among other things.

- Homeland Security Presidential Directive 5, "Management of Domestic Incidents," February 28, 2003, makes the Secretary of Homeland Security "the principal Federal official for domestic incident management," makes the Secretary "responsible for coordinating Federal operations within the United States to prepare for, respond to, and recover from terrorist attacks, major disasters, and other emergencies," and directs the Secretary to coordinate with private and nongovernmental sectors.[161] The directive further directs the Secretary to develop and administer a National Incident Management System (NIMS) to "provide a consistent nationwide approach for Federal, State, and local governments to work effectively and efficiently together to prepare for, respond to, and recover from domestic incidents, regardless of cause, size, or complexity" and to develop and administer a National Response Plan to "integrate Federal Government domestic prevention, preparedness, response, and recovery plans into one all-discipline, all-hazards plan."[162]

- The National Response Framework (NRF), which supersedes the National Response Plan, "presents the guiding principles that enable all response partners

---

[160] U.S. Department of Homeland Security. Federal Emergency Management Agency. "Robert T. Stafford Disaster Relief and Emergency Assistance Act (P.L. 93-288) as amended," http://www.fema.gov/about/stafact.shtm.

[161] For text of this and other Homeland Security Presidential Directives, see U.S. Department of Homeland Security, "Homeland Security Presidential Directives," http://www.dhs.gov/xabout/laws/editorial_0607.shtm.

[162] For further information on the National Incident Management System, see U.S. Department of Homeland Security. Federal Emergency Management Agency. "NIMS Resource Center," http://www.fema.gov/emergency/nims/.

to prepare for and provide a unified national response to disasters and emergencies—from the smallest incident to the largest catastrophe. The *Framework* establishes a comprehensive, national, all-hazards approach to domestic incident response."[163]

- The Post-Katrina Emergency Management Reform Act of 2006 (P.L. 109-296, Title VI) directs the FEMA Administrator to "lead the Nation's efforts to prepare for, protect against, respond to, recover from, and mitigate against the risk of natural disasters, acts of terrorism, and other man-made disasters, including catastrophic incidents," and to "develop a Federal response capability that, when necessary and appropriate, can act effectively and rapidly to deliver assistance essential to saving lives or protecting or preserving property or public health and safety in a natural disaster, act of terrorism, or other man-made disaster," among other things.

For further information on NRF, see CRS Report RL34758, *The National Response Framework: Overview and Possible Issues for Congress*, by Bruce R. Lindsay. For further information on the Stafford Act, see CRS Report RL33053, *Federal Stafford Act Disaster Assistance: Presidential Declarations, Eligible Activities, and Funding*, by Francis X. McCarthy.

The NRF has annexes for emergency support functions (e.g., communications, firefighting, public health), support (e.g., financial management, international coordination, public affairs), and incident types (e.g., biological, cyber, food and agriculture). The annex relevant to RDDs is the Nuclear/Radiological Incident Annex.[164] It "describes the policies, situations, concepts of operations, and responsibilities of the Federal departments and agencies governing the immediate response and short-term recovery activities for incidents involving release of radioactive materials."[165] It spells out which agency would have the lead ("coordinating agency") or would provide support ("cooperating agencies") in various incidents, and the capabilities and responsibilities of each. According to the Framework, DHS would be the coordinating agency for "all deliberate attacks involving nuclear/radiological facilities or materials, including RDDs or INDs."[166] The annex lists 11 key federal assets for nuclear or radiological incidents and how they are to be activated. Assets include:[167]

- Federal Radiological Monitoring and Assessment Center (FRMAC) "is responsible for coordinating all environmental radiological monitoring, sampling, and assessment activities for the response." DOE would lead FRMAC for the initial response; EPA would lead it for site cleanup.

- DOE Aerial Measuring System (AMS) uses aircraft to characterize radiation on the ground. The aircraft could, for example, "map large areas of contamination."

- DOE National Atmospheric Release Advisory Center (NARAC), operated by Lawrence Livermore National Laboratory, "provides real-time computer

---

[163] For further information on the National Response Framework, see U.S. Department of Homeland Security. Federal Emergency Management Agency. "NRF Resource Center," http://www.fema.gov/emergency/nrf/.
[164] For text of this annex, see http://www.fema.gov/pdf/emergency/nrf/nrf_nuclearradiologicalincidentannex.pdf.
[165] U.S. Department of Homeland Security. Federal Emergency Management Agency. "Nuclear/Radiological Incident Annex," June 2008, p. NUC-1, http://www.fema.gov/pdf/emergency/nrf/nrf_nuclearradiologicalincidentannex.pdf.
[166] Ibid., p. NUC-9.
[167] Federal Emergency Management Agency, "Nuclear/Radiological Incident Annex," pp. NUC-14 to NUC-16.

predictions of the atmospheric transport of material from radioactive releases and of the downwind effects on health and safety."[168]

- Interagency Modeling and Atmospheric Assessment Center (IMAAC) "provides the single Federal atmospheric prediction of hazardous material concentration to all levels of the Incident Command. ... The NARAC is the interim IMAAC." [169]

- DOE Radiological Assistance Program (RAP) Teams "provide first-responder radiological assistance to protect the health and safety of the general public, responders, and the environment, and to assist in the detection, identification and analysis, and response to events involving radiological/nuclear material."

- Advisory Team for Environment, Food, and Health "develops coordinated advice and recommendations on environmental, food, health, and animal health matters."

In August 2008, FEMA issued its "Planning Guidance for Protection and Recovery Following Radiological Dispersal Device (RDD) and Improvised Nuclear Device (IND) Incidents," which provides detailed guidance on response.[170]

Several agencies offer courses and exercises to aid with planning and response. For example, the DHS-sponsored TOPOFF (top officials) 4, held in October 2007, simulated an RDD attack on Portland, Oregon, Phoenix, Arizona, and Guam. It involved more than 15,000 federal, state, territorial, and local participants, requiring coordination between agencies at many levels of government.[171] [172] FEMA's National Training and Education Division offers hundreds of courses for first responders and emergency managers, some of which are offered through the National Domestic Preparedness Consortium, which FEMA sponsors. According to FEMA, over 60 of these courses specifically address nuclear and radiological incidents.[173] In addition, "GTRI has partnered with NNSA's Office of the Under Secretary for Counterterrorism and the FBI's Weapons of Mass Destruction Directorate to provide table top exercises at select nuclear and radiological sites. The purpose is to provide a no-fault, site-specific scenario where senior managers from various Federal, State, and municipal organizations can exercise their crisis management and consequence management skills in response to a terrorist incident."[174]

---

[168] For further information on NARAC, see Lawrence Livermore National Laboratory, "National Atmospheric Release Advisory Center," https://narac.llnl.gov/.

[169] The U.S. Interagency Modeling and Atmospheric Assessment Center home page is https://imaacweb.llnl.gov/web/signIn.html;jsessionid=6057C14752344F9D7A37A4F58A0ABBD4.

[170] U.S. Department of Homeland Security. Federal Emergency Management Agency. "Planning Guidance for Protection and Recovery Following Radiological Dispersal Device (RDD) and Improvised Nuclear Device (IND) Incidents," notice of final guidance, in U.S. National Archives and Records Administration. Office of the Federal Register. *Federal Register*, vol. 73, no. 149, August 1, 2008. pp. 45029-45048.

[171] U.S. Department of Homeland Security. "The TOPOFF 4 Full-Scale Exercise." http://www.dhs.gov/files/training/gc_1179430526487.shtm, page last reviewed or modified August 31, 2009.

[172] These exercises are now called National Level Exercises. For further information, see CRS Report RL34737, *Homeland Emergency Preparedness and the National Exercise Program: Background, Policy Implications, and Issues for Congress*, coordinated by R. Eric Petersen.

[173] Information provided by FEMA through DHS, email, May 4, 2010. The website for FEMA's National Training and Education Division is https://www firstrespondertraining.gov/TEI/tei.do?a=home, and for the National Domestic Preparedness Consortium, http://www.ndpc.us/.

[174] "Prepared Statement of Kenneth Sheely," p. 17.

U.S. planning for response also has an international component. For example, according to the State Department,

> The Foreign Emergency Support Team is the United States Government's only interagency, on-call, short-notice team poised to respond to terrorist incidents worldwide. Led and trained by the Operations Directorate of the Office of the Coordinator for Counterterrorism, it assists U.S. missions and host governments in responding quickly and effectively to terrorist attacks. The FEST, which has deployed to over 20 countries since its inception in 1986, leaves for an incident site within four hours of notification, providing the fastest assistance possible. [75]

In addition to federal planning, some states and localities have developed response plans and held exercises. New York City created a Counterterrorism Bureau in 2002, which addresses chemical, biological, radiological, nuclear, and explosive threats.[176] Washington, DC, adopted NIMS in 2005.[177] Missouri held an exercise in August 2005 simulating response to an RDD attack involving coordination between state and local participants. In Kansas City, participating departments included "Emergency Management, Fire, Police, Health, Water Services, City Manager's Office, City Communications, Public Works, and Parks and Recreation."[178] In June 2008, the West Virginia Homeland Security Department ran an exercise in which a dirty bomb hit Washington, DC, and thousands of people fled to West Virginia. The exercise tested the ability of state and local emergency personnel to respond to this scenario.[179] On April 26-30, 2010, EPA, the Pennsylvania Department of Environmental Protection, and the City of Philadelphia sponsored "Liberty RadEx," an exercise involving over 700 federal, state, and local personnel "to test the country's capability to clean up and help communities recover from a dirty bomb terrorist attack."[180] This exercise focused on recovery as distinct from response.

Efforts of governments at all levels to spell out agency responsibilities, develop response plans, stockpile supplies, and conduct exercises are intended to help respond to an RDD attack. At issue for any disaster plan is how well it would work in practice. While the answer is unknowable beforehand, response plans have functioned poorly in many types of disasters or analysts have questioned their adequacy. An assessment of state radiation emergency preparedness found, "in almost every measure of public health capacity and capability, the public health system remains poorly prepared to adequately respond to a major radiation emergency incident."[181] A press report found, "Many states do not have a basic radiation emergency plan for communicating with the

---

[175] U.S. Department of State. Office of the Coordinator for Counterterrorism. "Foreign Emergency Support Team (FEST)." http://www.state.gov/s/ct/about/c16664 htm.

[176] New York City. Police Department. "Counterterrorism Units." http://www nyc.gov/html/nypd/html/administration/counterterrorism_units.shtml.

[177] Washington, DC, Homeland Security and Emergency Management, "National Incident Management System (NIMS)," http://hsema.dc.gov/dcema/cwp/view,a,1226,q,636296,dcemaNav,%7C31808%7C,.asp.

[178] City of Kansas City, MO, "Dirty Bomb Exercise Aug. 17 Will Test City's Preparedness," press release, August 16, 2005, http://ww4 kcmo.org/cco nsf/10ba38b6a738836b8625708f004cbf95/72f03a3b691c1f8c8625705f005a9aab?OpenDocument.

[179] Cecelia Mason, "Dirty Bomb Exercise Tests West Virginia's Emergency Services," West Virginia Public Broadcasting, June 18, 2008, http://www.wvpubcast.org/newsarticle.aspx?id=2822.

[180] U.S. Environmental Protection Agency. Region 3. "Liberty RadEx Drill to Test National Clean-up and Recovery Efforts after Mock 'Dirty Bomb' Attack," news release, April 26, 2010, http://yosemite.epa.gov/opa/admpress nsf/90829d899627a1d98525735900400c2b/28c5b280d311903a8525771100525103!OpenDocument.

[181] Council of State and Territorial Epidemiologists, "The Status of State-Level Radiation Emergency Preparedness and Response Capabilities, 2010," October 6, 2010, p. 13, http://www.cste.org/webpdfs/2010raditionreport.pdf.

---

public or responding to the health risks."[182] The response to Hurricane Katrina was poor despite decades of planning, and the response to the Gulf oil spill was poor despite legislation providing for the National Oil and Hazardous Substances Pollution Contingency Plan.[183] At a hearing in 2008, Irwin Redlener, M.D., Director, National Center for Disaster Preparedness, Columbia University, said, "few if any major U.S. urban centers have taken on the admittedly daunting challenge of planning for a meaningful public health response to a nuclear detonation, even if they've actively and effectively planned for other natural or terror-related disasters."[184] And the Commission on the Prevention of Weapons of Mass Destruction Proliferation and Terrorism, in its 2010 report card, gave the United States an "F" on "enhanc[ing] the nation's capabilities for rapid response to prevent biological attacks from inflicting mass casualties."[185]

Response

FEMA's "Planning Guidance for Protection and Recovery Following Radiological Dispersal Device (RDD) and Improvised Nuclear Device (IND) Incidents" divides response into early, intermediate, and late phases, as noted under "Radiation and Its Effects." The source of resources would shift with the phase. In the early phase, which would begin when it was determined that an RDD attack had occurred, state and local first responders would be the primary ones available. They would focus on minimizing deaths and injuries from radiation and panic. Authorities could do this by implementing rescue and evacuation plans, taking steps to minimize panic, providing information on personal protection measures, caring for evacuees, providing medical care for those who may have been exposed to high levels of radiation, and decontaminating large numbers of people.

The intermediate phase response could begin in as little as a few hours after an attack. It would involve higher-level care for those suffering from radiation injuries, longer-term relocation of people from areas with dangerous levels of radioactivity, and initial stages of recovery, such as decontaminating and returning to service water supply, roads, and other critical infrastructure affected by the attack. Many federal resources could be brought to bear in the intermediate phase. but it should not be assumed that this would happen promptly. Irwin Redlener of Columbia University, pointed to "the myth of federal rescue" in the event of a nuclear attack. He observed that the public and disaster planners alike believe that federal help would be available within a few hours regardless of the catastrophe, but that "relatively few assets can be expected to provide timely, very large-scale medical triage, major hospital care and so forth."[186]

Federal resources, in addition to those discussed earlier, include:

---

[182] Sherri Fink, "U.S. Health-Care Systems Said to Be Unprepared for Nuclear Disaster" *Washington Post,* March 8, 2011, p. 3.

[183] Laws expanding this plan include the Federal Water Pollution Control Act of 1972 (Clean Water Act), P.L. 92-500; Comprehensive Environmental Response, Compensation, and Liability Act of 1980 (Superfund), P.L. 96-510; and the Oil Pollution Act of 1990, P.L. 101-380. See U.S. Environmental Protection Agency. "National Oil and Hazardous Substances Pollution Contingency Plan Overview," http://www.epa.gov/oem/content/lawsregs/ncpover.htm.

[184] U.S. Congress. Senate. Committee on Homeland Security and Governmental Affairs. *Nuclear Terrorism: Providing Medical Care and Meeting Basic Needs in the Aftermath,* hearing, 110th Congress, 2nd Session, May 15, 2008.

[185] Commission on the Prevention of Weapons of Mass Destruction Proliferation and Terrorism. "Report Card: Government Failing to Protect America from Grave Threats of WMD Proliferation and Terrorism." January 26, 2010, http://www.preventwmd.org/1_26_101/.

[186] U.S. Congress. Senate. Committee on Homeland Security and Governmental Affairs. *Nuclear Terrorism: Providing Medical Care and Meeting Basic Needs in the Aftermath,* hearing, 110th Congress, 2nd Session, May 15, 2008.

- Pre-Positioned Equipment Program (PEP) Pods: "FEMA maintains geographically dispersed caches of first responder equipment in 'PEP' Pods that are rapidly deployable to augment first responder capabilities for all-hazards events. PEP pods consist of personal protective equipment, decontamination equipment, detection instruments, search and rescue equipment, logistics equipment, and interoperable communications capabilities."[187]

- Emergency Support: The Nuclear Emergency Support Team (NEST), operated by the National Nuclear Security Administration, is that agency's "program for preparing and equipping specialized response teams to deal with the technical aspects of nuclear or radiological terrorism. NEST capabilities include search and identification of nuclear materials, diagnostics and assessment of suspected nuclear devices, technical operations in support of render safe procedures, and packaging for transport to final disposition."[188] The Radiation Emergency Assistance Center/Training Site, managed by the Oak Ridge Institute for Science and Education, has staff who "are available 24 hours a day/7 days a week to deploy and provide emergency medical consultation for incidents involving radiation anywhere in the world."[189]

- Medical Stockpile: The Centers for Disease Control and Prevention, an agency of the Department of Health and Human Services, operates the Strategic National Stockpile, a national repository of medical supplies that is "designed to supplement and resupply state and local public health agencies in the event of a national emergency anywhere and at anytime within the United States or its territories."[190] This stockpile maintains supplies of several agents of use for medical problems arising from a radiological or nuclear attack. For example, prussian blue, a medical form of a blue dye, is highly effective for eliminating cesium and thallium from the body, including for cesium-137 contamination.[191] The Project BioShield Act of 2004 (P.L. 108-276) established Project BioShield. Its purpose "is to accelerate the research, development, purchase, and availability of effective medical countermeasures for the adverse health effects of chemical, biological, radiological, and nuclear (CBRN) agents."[192] HHS contracted with

---

[187] Information provided by Department of Homeland Security, May 4, 2010.

[188] U.S. Department of Energy. National Nuclear Security Administration. Nevada Site Office. "Nuclear Emergency Support Team (NEST)," http://www nv.doe.gov/nationalsecurity/homelandsecurity/nest htm. For further detail, see U.S. Department of Energy. National Nuclear Security Administration. "Nuclear Emergency Support Team (NEST)," http://www.nv.doe.gov/library/FactSheets/NEST.pdf.

[189] Oak Ridge Institute for Science and Education, "Radiation Emergency Assistance Center/Training Site (REAC/TS)," http://orise.orau.gov/reacts/.

[190] U.S. Department of Health and Human Services. "Radiological Event Medical Management: Strategic National Stockpile (SNS)," http://www.remm.nlm.gov/sns.htm#agents.

[191] U.S. Department of Health and Human Services. "Radiological Event Medical Management: Prussian Blue (Radiogardase ®)," http://www.remm.nlm.gov/prussianblue htm; and U.S. Department of Health and Human Services. Centers for Disease Control and Prevention. "Emergency Preparedness and Response: Prussian Blue," fact sheet, http://www.bt.cdc.gov/radiation/prussianblue.asp.

[192] U.S. Department of Health and Human Services. Assistant Secretary for Preparedness and Response. "Project BioShield," http://www hhs.gov/aspr/barda/mcm/radiologicalthreats.html. See also CRS Report R41033, *Project BioShield: Authorities, Appropriations, Acquisitions, and Issues for Congress*, by Frank Gottron; and U.S. Department of Health and Human Services. Assistant Secretary for Preparedness and Response. National Biodefense Safety Board. *Where Are the Countermeasures? Protecting America's Health from CBRN Threats*, March 2010, http://www.phe.gov/Preparedness/legal/boards/nbsb/meetings/Documents/nbsb-mcmreport.pdf

Akorn, Inc., in 2006 for 475,000 doses of pharmaceuticals to treat internal contamination by radioactive particles.[193]

- Dose measurement: Following an RDD attack, some people would likely be exposed to radiation, and many more would be concerned that they were so exposed. Treatment of radiological exposure would depend on the dose an individual received. Dose can be measured by examining blood for chromosome damage, but current methods could reportedly process only a few hundred persons a day by sending blood samples to laboratories. Columbia University scientists are developing automated equipment for the purpose; each unit could potentially determine the dose for some 30,000 persons per day. This research is being funded by the National Institute of Allergy and Infectious Diseases and the Biomedical Advanced Research and Development Authority, both units of the Department of Health and Human Services.[194] The Armed Forces Radiobiology Research Institute has a Biodosimetry Assessment Tool, "a computer-based software diagnostic tool for use by health-care providers early after a radiation incident. Assists providers in identifying individuals with significant radiation exposures and in making appropriate treatment decisions."[195]

The Department of Defense (DOD) has a Chemical, Biological, Radiological, and Nuclear (CBRN) response enterprise that, upon approval by the Secretary of Defense, would come under the operational control of the Commander, U.S. Northern Command. This enterprise maintains several levels of assets to respond to any type of such attack in the United States.[196] Many of these would be brought to bear in the intermediate phase. In the case of an RDD attack, the DOD asset most likely to arrive on the scene first is the WMD Civil Support Team (CST), operated by the National Guard. As of June 2011, California and New York had two CSTs apiece that were certified as operationally ready, while territories, the District of Columbia, and other states each had one, for a total of 56. DOD expects a second CST in Florida to be certified by the end of FY2011. Each team has 22 National Guard personnel. CSTs deploy at the direction of the governor of the affected state within 3 hours of notification. They have equipment to identify radioactive materials, can assess consequences of an attack, and can advise incident command personnel on response measures. The next level of response is the Chemical, Biological, Radiological, Nuclear, and High-Yield Explosive (CBRNE) Enhanced Response Force Package, or CERFP, also a National Guard asset. There are 17 in the United States, one or more for each of the ten FEMA regions. Each has about 170 personnel with a response time of 6 to 12 hours, and has medical, search and extraction, and decontamination personnel. The third level of response is the Homeland Response Forces (HRFs), for which planning is underway. There are to be ten, one

---

[193] CRS, *Project BioShield,* section titled "Acquisitions."

[194] Lisa Foderaro, "Columbia Scientists Prepare for a Threat: A Dirty Bomb," *New York Times,* July 8, 2010. For more detail, see Guy Garty et al., "The RABIT: A Rapid Automated Biosimetry Tool for Radiological Triage," *Health Physics,* vol. 98, no. 2, February 2010, pp. 209-217, http://www.mrl.columbia.edu/Guy-HealthPhysics-2010.pdf.

[195] U.S. Department of Defense. Uniformed Services University of the Health Sciences. Armed Forces Radiobiology Research Institute. "Biodosimetry Tools," http://www.afrri.usuhs.mil/outreach/biodostools.htm#software.

[196] Information in this paragraph provided by Chemical, Biological, Radiological, and Nuclear Directorate, Office of Homeland Defense Integration and Defense Support of Civil Authorities, Office of the Secretary of Defense, Department of Defense, personal communications, September 15 and 22, 2010, and February 14 and June 6, 2011; and U.S. National Guard. "WMD CST," fact sheet, current as of November 9, 2009, 1 p., http://www.ng.mil/features/HomelandDefense/cst/CST_Fact_Sheet.pdf; U.S. National Guard. "CERFP," fact sheet, current as of May 21, 2007, 1 p., http://www.ng.mil/features/HomelandDefense/cerfp/CERFP_Fact_Sheet.doc; and U.S. Department of Defense. "Homeland Response Force (HRF) Fact Sheet" (2 p.) and "CBRNE Enhanced Response Force Package (CERFP) Fact Sheet" (1 p.), http://www.defense.gov/news/HRFCERFP.pdf.

---

for each FEMA region. They are to stand up throughout FY2011 and FY2012. Each is to have about 570 National Guard personnel, divided among medical, search and extraction, decontamination, security, and command and control teams; response time is to be 6 to 12 hours. Finally, there are federal assets, currently in the form of two CBRNE Consequence Management Response Force (CCMRF) units. Each has about 4,700 personnel. CCMRF 1 is primarily an active component force, while CCMRF 2 is made up of reserve personnel. Each provides logistical support as well as medical, search and rescue, and decontamination assets, and would deploy for very large incidents. As of June 2011, DOD was phasing out the two CCMRFs and replacing them with one Defense CBRN Response Force (DCRF), which is to have 5,200 personnel drawn from the Army, Army Reserve, Marines, and Air Force. Like the CCMRF, the DCRF will have capability in such areas as medevac, surgery, logistics, engineering, and airlift; will have more capability than CERFPs and HRFs in medical care and in search and extraction from contaminated environments; and will have enhanced equipment and training. The CBRN response enterprise also includes two Command and Control CBRN Response Elements (C2CREs) to provide command, control, and communications support to contingency follow-on forces as needed.

A DOD agency, the Defense Threat Reduction Agency (DTRA), operates Technical Support Groups, which are rapidly deployable teams of military, scientific, and technical personnel. These groups can assist in the search and recovery of RDDs and nuclear weapons, and have a reachback capability through the DTRA Operations Center to link to numerous government subject matter experts.[197]

Recovery

Late-phase efforts would focus on recovery. The goal would be to restore human activity in the affected area to preattack levels insofar as possible. The main activity would be reduction of radiation hazards to an acceptable level, such as by decontaminating streets and buildings, demolishing and replacing buildings that cannot be cost-effectively decontaminated, or declaring certain areas to be off limits. FEMA does not provide PAGs for cleanup in the late phase:

> Because of the extremely broad range of potential impacts that may occur from RDDs and INDs ... a pre-established numeric cleanup guideline is not recommended as best serving the needs of decision makers in the late phase. Rather, a process should be used to determine the societal objectives for expected land uses and the options and approaches available, in order to select the most acceptable criteria.... Late phase cleanup criteria should be derived through a site-specific optimization process, which should include potential future land uses, technical feasibility, costs, cost-effectiveness, and public acceptability.[198]

The reason for site-specific optimization is that cleanup requirements would depend on details of the attack:

- What radioactive material or materials were used? Materials differ in how they bond to surfaces and thus on what techniques must be used to remove them. The form of material affects how it disperses.

---

[197] Information provided by Defense Threat Reduction Agency, personal communication, September 28, 2010.
[198] Federal Emergency Management Agency, "Planning Guidance for Protection and Recovery Following Radiological Dispersal Device (RDD) and Improvised Nuclear Device (IND) Incidents," *Federal Register,* August 1, 2008, p. 45036.

- What type of device was used? An explosive-driven device might increase the area over which radioactive material is spread while reducing the amount of material per unit of area; material spread over a smaller area would make for more intense radioactivity in that area; and material released inside a building might make that building uninhabitable.

- What was the weather? A strong wind could disperse the material over a wider area, wind direction would affect where the material goes, and rain would rinse it out of the air and into storm sewers and bodies of water. Rain might cause some materials to penetrate into city surfaces, or wash away other materials.

- Where is the material? The cleanup plan would need to take into account the importance of contaminated areas, as well as the difficulty of decontaminating them.

Recovery from an RDD attack would require many state and local resources, and localities are best positioned to determine which areas merit highest priority for remediation. Yet few states and cities are likely to have the financial and technical resources to draw up site-specific recovery plans and stockpile the necessary supplies and equipment, and generic plans might be of little value because they would not reflect details of the attack. Thus, federal agencies would probably provide detailed planning and specialized resources after an attack.

The Post-Katrina Emergency Management Reform Act of 2006 (P.L. 109-296) dealt with recovery. Section 202 mandated that FEMA, in coordination with other agencies, "shall develop, coordinate, and maintain a National Disaster Recovery Strategy." In keeping with this mandate, in September 2009 President Obama directed the establishment of the White House Long-Term Disaster Recovery Working Group, co-chaired by the Secretaries of Homeland Security and Housing and Urban Development and involving the heads of more than 20 federal agencies.[199] According to FEMA, the working group will deliver two strategic planning documents.[200] The National Disaster Recovery Framework will provide an overarching strategy for how the U.S. government deals with all aspects of recovery, from short-term to long-term, from disasters of all types and sizes.[201] As of June 2011, the framework document was undergoing interagency review. Once it has been reviewed by the interagency and all comments are resolved, it will go to the White House for approval and publication. The working group will also deliver a report focusing on long-term response to large disasters, including such aspects as dealing with societal consequences, restoration of infrastructure, and economic development. As of June 2011, this report was moving through the concurrence process (i.e., agreement among the organizations drafting the report) and will be ready for interagency review soon. After that, it will go to the White House for approval and publication. There is no target release date for either document.

A 2010 GAO report raised questions about the adequacy of preparations for recovery. GAO found that "FEMA, the DHS agency responsible for developing a comprehensive emergency management system, has not developed a national disaster recovery strategy, as required by law, or issued specific guidance to coordinate federal, state, and local government recovery planning

---

[199] See U.S. White House. Long-Term Disaster Recovery Working Group. "Purpose Statement." http://www.disasterrecoveryworkinggroup.gov/purpose-statement.cfm.

[200] Information in the balance of this paragraph was provided by FEMA, personal communication, June 14, 2011.

[201] See U.S. White House. Long-Term Disaster Recovery Working Group. *National Disaster Recovery Framework*. Draft, February 5, 2010, p. 2, http://www.disasterrecoveryworkinggroup.gov/ndrf.pdf.

for RDD and IND incidents, as directed by executive guidance."[202] However, the Nuclear/Radiological Incident Annex of the NRF provides guidance for response and short-term recovery; the FEMA "Planning Guidance for Protection and Recovery Following Radiological Dispersal Device (RDD) and Improvised Nuclear Device (IND) Incidents" provides a framework for longer-term recovery; and the Long-Term Disaster Recovery Working Group is preparing detailed guidance and recommendations.

There has been some research into decontamination. One study found that for radioactive materials like cesium that bond with concrete and tile, washing with water would have little effect.[203] Worse, "the penetration of the solution [water carrying radioactive material] into the material [concrete, tile] … may be followed by the virtually irreversible fixation of the dissolved elements."[204] The report found a solution of water with ammonium oxalate or ammonium chloride to be more effective than water.[205] However, ammonium oxalate is "very poisonous by ingestion and inhalation," corrosive to mucous membranes, and may cause severe irritation to skin and eyes.[206] Ammonium chloride "causes irritation to skin, eyes and respiratory tract" and is "harmful if swallowed or inhaled."[207] An R&D project at Idaho National Laboratory is investigating the use of lasers for decontamination. The process envisions wetting surfaces so water would reach into the pores (such as in concrete) holding radioactive material, and using the heat from the laser to turn water into steam, bringing the radioactive material to the surface where it could be washed away.[208] Argonne National Laboratory is developing a "supergel" intended "to safely capture and dispose of radioactive elements in porous structures outdoors, such as buildings and monuments, using a spray-on, super-absorbent gel and engineered nanoparticles," for use in the event of an RDD attack.[209] EPA's National Homeland Security Research Center conducts research on decontamination.[210] The center cautions that decontamination is complex:

> EPA has found that studies done in the laboratory using small samples of materials (coupons) are difficult to apply to large scale decontamination problems; likewise, decontamination systems designed to use in large spaces are difficult to adapt to small test chambers. … Studies have shown that there is no universal decontamination approach. The effectiveness of a decontamination technology (efficacy) largely depends on the contaminated material type. What works well on one surface type contaminated with one agent does not necessarily work on a different surface with the same agent. In addition, the concentration of the decontaminant, the contact time of the decontaminant with the material,

---

[202] U.S. Government Accountability Office, *Combating Nuclear Terrorism: Actions Needed to Better Prepare to Recover from Possible Attacks Using Radiological or Nuclear Materials*, GAO-10-204, January 2010, highlights page, http://www.gao.gov/new.items/d10204.pdf.

[203] J. Real et al., "Mechanisms of Desorption of 134Cs [cesium-134] and 85Sr [strontium-85] Aerosols Deposited on Urban Surfaces," *Journal of Environmental Radioactivity,* 62 (2002), p. 1.

[204] Ibid., p. 7.

[205] Ibid., p. 1.

[206] Mallinckrodt Baker, Inc., "Material Safety Data Sheet: Ammonium Oxalate," http://www.jtbaker.com/msds/englishhtml/a6072 htm.

[207] Mubychem Group, "Ammonium Chloride Manufacturers—MSDS [Material Safety Data Sheet]," http://mubychem.com/MSDS/ammonium_chloride%20MSDS htm.

[208] Mike Wall, "INL Laser Research Could Help U.S. Respond to Terror Attack," April 19, 2010, https://inlportal.inl.gov/portal/server.pt?open=514&objID=1269&mode=2&featurestory=DA_547419.

[209] Argonne National Laboratory. "'Supergel' System for Cleaning Radioactively Contaminated Structures," http://www.anl.gov/techtransfer/Available_Technologies/Chemistry/supergel.html.

[210] U.S. Environmental Protection Agency. Homeland Security Research. http://www.epa.gov/nhsrc/. The center's reports on RDDs are available at http://tinyurl.com/3kfyntf.

---

and conditions such as temperature, sunlight, or relative humidity all affect decontaminant efficacy.[211]

Time could be of the essence for fluid decontamination because of the need to apply chemicals before rain, or even humidity, caused "virtually irreversible fixation of the dissolved elements." Would the chemicals and equipment needed for fluid decontamination be available promptly? While the waste fluid could be stored temporarily, it would have to be treated because it would be hazardous. Possible methods to remove contaminants from water include an activated charcoal waste water system or a reverse osmosis system. Could they be deployed soon enough to support decontamination efforts? The potential of a radionuclide to bond with other material like concrete depends on the radionuclide and on its chemical form. Some radionuclides bond more readily with concrete than others, and a radionuclide that is strongly bonded in a chemical compound may be unable to break that bond to bond with another substance. "First decontaminators" would benefit by knowing what material was used in an attack.

Also at issue are how quickly laboratory-scale processes could be scaled up to produce the enormous quantities of decontamination chemicals that might be needed following an RDD attack, how the waste stream from decontamination (chemicals, water, radioactive material, other materials) would be handled, how decontamination workers would be protected against radiation and hazardous chemicals, and the relative cost-effectiveness of decontamination vs. demolition and reconstruction.

Decontamination must be done to a level that provides safety. But how safe is safe enough? The question is intensely practical. There are major tradeoffs between the level of decontamination required and the cost, time, technology, and effort needed to achieve each level. As illustrated by the attack specified in **Figure 3**, the cost to clean up and rebuild varies greatly with the cleanup level required, ranging from a few billion dollars (Canadian) for a level of 500 mrem/year to about C$70 billion for a level of 15 mrem/year. Conversely, accepting a slightly higher level of contamination, and a slightly higher risk of cancers, could make the difference between declaring large urban areas off-limits for years or permitting their use.

Attribution

In addition to taking steps to minimize the consequences of an attack, the United States would surely want to retaliate against the perpetrators. Retaliation would require identifying the source of material and perpetrator of an attack in a process known as attribution. Attribution relies on a fusion of evidence from intelligence, law enforcement, and scientific analysis of material from the weapon, a process known as forensics. A detailed discussion of how intelligence and law enforcement would contribute to attribution are beyond the scope of this report and may be classified; this section focuses on forensics.

Nuclear forensics analyzes debris from nuclear explosions, and has been conducted for many decades. A report on nuclear forensics stated, "During the first 50 years of the nuclear weapons era, radiochemistry techniques were developed and used to determine the characteristics (such as yield, materials used, and design details) of nuclear explosions carried out by the United States

---

[211] U.S. Environmental Protection Agency. Homeland Security Research. "Indoor and Outdoor Decontamination," http://www.epa.gov/nhsrc/aboutdecon html#iodra.

and by other countries."[212] Scientists could use such techniques to analyze minute samples of material from a terrorist nuclear weapon. Such materials may have trace amounts of impurities that provide signatures unique to a country or even a particular reactor. For example, highly enriched uranium picks up impurities from the area where the original natural uranium was mined, from equipment used to separate uranium-235 from uranium-238, and, if some of it was reprocessed, from a nuclear reactor. Weapons-grade plutonium picks up impurities from the reactor that produced it and from processes used to purify it. The detonation of a nuclear weapon generates "over 300 different isotopes of 36 elements,"[213] some of which have half-lives of hours or less. The variety of radionuclides, any impurities, and debris from the weapon's nonnuclear components would provide many clues to the weapon's origins.

Nuclear forensics uses various techniques. It matches samples of weapon material to an archive of samples from facilities producing such material, or against a library of information from manufacturers. (Government agencies use "archive" to refer to a collection of physical samples and "library" to refer to a collection of information.) It looks for clues that link to other types of evidence, such as records of missing material. It identifies manufacturing processes, and may use simulation to see if a certain process could have led to a certain sample. By providing information on weapon materials and design, forensics could help determine the technical sophistication of the terrorist group that launched a nuclear attack, and which nations, if any, provided technical support, materials, or even a weapon. The potential to identify the source of material and the perpetrator of an attack supports deterrence and, if deterrence failed, could support retaliation.

The United States is developing a consolidated library and archive of nuclear material:

> On August 28, 2006, the national-level Nuclear Materials Information Program (NMIP) was established via National and Homeland Security Presidential Directive (NSPD-48/HSPD-17). NMIP is an interagency effort managed by the Department of Energy's Office of Intelligence and Counterintelligence, in close coordination with the Departments of State, Defense, Homeland Security, Justice, the Nuclear Regulatory Commission, and agencies under the Director of National Intelligence.
>
> While the specifics of NMIP are classified, the goal of NMIP is to consolidate information from all sources pertaining to worldwide nuclear materials holdings and their security status into an integrated and continuously updated information management system. ... NMIP also is developing a national registry for identifying and tracking nuclear material samples that are held throughout the U.S. to support the information needs of the United States Government.[214]

DHS observed that technical nuclear forensics (TNF) assessments do not depend solely on physical comparison of samples. For example, "TNF may be able to link collected/interdicted material to types of manufacturing processes, facilities, and/or geographic locations, excluding

---

[212] Joint Working Group of the American Physical Society and the American Association for the Advancement of Science, *Nuclear Forensics: Role, State of the Art, and Program Needs,* 2008, p. 3, http://iis-db.stanford.edu/pubs/22126/APS_AAAS_2008.pdf.

[213] U.S. Department of Defense and Department of Energy. *The Effects of Nuclear Weapons,* third edition, compiled and edited by Samuel Glasstone and Philip Dolan. Washington, GPO, 1977, p. 633.

[214] "Statement of Rolf Mowatt-Larssen, Director of the Office of Intelligence and Counterintelligence, United States Department of Energy, before the Homeland Security and Governmental Affairs Committee, United States Senate, April 2, 2008," available via U.S. Congress. Senate. Committee on Homeland Security and Governmental Affairs. Hearings. "Nuclear Terrorism: Assessing the Threat to the Homeland," April 2, 2008, http://hsgac.senate.gov/public/index.cfm?FuseAction=Hearings.Hearing&Hearing_ID=42449878-5e68-4eef-978d-8e671fed2ab0.

possibilities along the way from further consideration and thus narrowing the range of possible candidates." Further, "TNF can also link collected/interdicted material to types of manufacturing and production processes through computational modeling and simulation. For example, computational modeling of production processes and their effects on the resulting materials would provide insight into distinguishing characteristics of nuclear materials. Predicted results can then be compared to the actual material to see if there is a match."[215]

Radiological forensics uses many of these techniques as well. It might be able to determine the age of a sample, which in turn might help eliminate some manufacturers as the source of the material.[216] In addition, as DHS states, "non-rad[ioactive] evidence associated with the RDD will play an important role in the technical forensics investigation, for both pre- and post-detonation. It is also important to note that, just as is the case for classical and nuclear forensics, with RDD forensics the ability to exclude candidate sources is very important to the overall investigation." Further, "material databases are only one type of 'clue.' Additional useful insights can be garnered from license information, sales records, vendor catalogs, etc., and this information is being collected as funding and accessibility allow."[217]

There are libraries of information on radioactive materials. For example, "The IAEA has developed the International Catalogue of Sealed Radioactive Sources and Devices (ICSRS) to become a comprehensive catalogue of manufacturer's data on sealed radioactive sources and the devices in which they are or can be used. The system includes data on sources, the devices housing the sources, and details of manufacturers and suppliers worldwide."[218] NRC maintains a Sealed Source and Device Registry (SS&DR), which lists such products approved for use by its licensees,[219] as well as the National Source Tracking System discussed earlier.

DHS said that since the vast majority of sealed sources are made in foreign countries, and many of them are not sold in the United States, it is funding Argonne National Laboratory (ANL) and Idaho National Laboratory (INL) to gather information about these sources "from discussions with manufacturers, irradiators, recyclers, and distributors under non-disclosure agreements; visits to manufacturing facilities; open-source data mining in the native language; and examination of international transport declarations. The information collected is deposited into an ANL/INL Sealed Source Database."[220] According to a 2010 INL report, the IAEA and NRC libraries were not intended for forensics.

> In contrast, the ANL/INL [Argonne National Laboratory/Idaho National Laboratory] Sealed Source Database was designed for forensics purposes, and so, in addition to all of the information contained in the US NRC SS&DR, it also contains commercial production information, trace element impurities, isotopic ratios, and other technical information, as available. While most model information pertains to sources and devices made or sold in the

---

[215] Information provided by Department of Homeland Security, personal communication, October 18, 2010.

[216] For example, when cesium-137 is purified from nuclear spent fuel, it typically contains a negligible amount of barium-137 (which is not radioactive). Over time, as cesium-137 decays into barium-137, the ratio of the two changes at a rate determined by the half-life of cesium-137. This ratio can be used to determine the age of the sample. Information provided by Department of Homeland Security, personal communication, October 14, 2010.

[217] Information provided by Department of Homeland Security, email, May 17, 2010

[218] International Atomic Energy Agency, "International Catalogue of Sealed Radioactive Sources and Devices ICSRS)," http://nucleus.iaea.org/CIR/CIR/ICSRS.html##.

[219] U.S. Nuclear Regulatory Commission."Sealed Source and Device Registry: Supplement for 10 CFR Part 35 Uses." http://www.nrc.gov/materials/miau/miau-reg-initiatives/ssd-registry html.

[220] Personal communication, Department of Homeland Security, February 25, 2011.

US, considerable effort has been expended to include comparable information about foreign-made sources and devices. At this time, the ANL/INL Sealed Source Database is the most extensive and detailed catalog of sealed source models in the world. However, even it is considered a "work in progress," with additional information being continuously included.[221]

While there are libraries of data, there does not appear to be an archive of radioactive sources or materials. While it is impossible to prove a negative, communications in 2011 with knowledgeable individuals at DOE, NNSA, the Domestic Nuclear Detection Office of DHS, NRC, Los Alamos National Laboratory, Lawrence Livermore National Laboratory, and Sandia National Laboratories indicated that these organizations had no archive of samples of radioactive material or sealed sources.

Radiological forensics differs from nuclear forensics in various ways, as **Table 1** shows. Some differences are technical. A nuclear explosion produces hundreds of radionuclides; materials that might be used in an RDD, excepting spent fuel, would likely have one or a few radionuclides, providing fewer clues. RDD radionuclides have half-lives measured in years, not hours or less, so collecting samples would not be as time-urgent as for a nuclear explosion. Other differences are political. Nuclear forensics could support retaliation, depending on the country of origin of the material. (It is almost inconceivable that the United States would retaliate against Russia following an IND attack; retaliation against some other nations is plausible.) Radiological forensics would probably not support retaliation. RDD material might be produced in one country, distributed by a second, sold to a third, and perhaps resold to a fourth, where terrorists might steal it. Argentina, Canada, several European countries, and Russia are the main producers of key radionuclides,[222] which they sell in legitimate commercial transactions, so tracing material to the producer would not provide a basis for retaliation. If terrorists obtained material through theft, illicit purchase, or an inside job, it would be hard to assign malevolent intent to the country involved. Tracing material to the end user country might thus be of little value for retaliation.

Postdetonation forensics would analyze clues from the radioactive material and weapon debris. Predetonation forensics, i.e., with access to the device, could glean far more information because standard crime lab techniques could obtain clues from the device in addition to clues from the radioactive materials. Predetonation clues would include characteristics of the radioactive material, including its chemical form and any matrix material in which it was embedded; weapon design; characteristics of the casing, detonator, and chemical explosives; and fingerprints, footprints, pieces of fabric, strands of hair, and similar evidence from the scene. Another advantage of predetonation forensics is that trace impurities would be much easier to detect, as they would be concentrated in the device rather than diluted over a large area. As a result, predetonation forensics could increase the likelihood of attribution.

---

[221] Margaret Goldberg and Martha Finck, "International Data on Radiological Sources," Idaho National Laboratory, INL/CON-10-18939, Preprint, July 2010, p. 3, http://www.inl.gov/technicalpublications/Documents/4633185.pdf.

[222] National Research Council. *Radiation Source Use and Replacement, Abbreviated Version*, p. 41.

Table 1. Differences Between Nuclear and Radiological Forensics

	Nuclear Forensics	Radiological Forensics
Link between forensics, attribution, and retaliation	Nuclear materials are tightly guarded and may contain unique clues. Forensic analysis might point strongly to the perpetrator, supporting high-confidence attribution that could lead directly to retaliation. This would not be the case if the material were stolen from certain nations such as Russia.	Radiological materials are distributed worldwide, and may have little security. Clues may point to the country of manufacture but not to the perpetrator of an attack, so that the material by itself may provide few clues to support attribution or retaliation.
Number and type of radionuclides used in device	Several: uranium-235, plutonium (mix of isotopes), deuterium, tritium (hydrogen isotopes)	Most likely one unless spent fuel is used. Possibilities include cesium-137, cobalt-60, iridium-192, americium-241
Would forensics support retaliation?	Perhaps, depending on country	Probably not
Predetonation and postdetonation radionuclides the same?	A nuclear explosion creates many new radionuclides	An RDD, even if explosive-driven, disperses materials but does not change its radionuclides
Technical importance of prompt acquisition of postdetonation samples	Very important; a nuclear explosion produces many radionuclides with very short half-lives	Not important; radionuclides most likely to be used in an RDD have half-lives measured in years
Number of radionuclides available for postdetonation analysis	Several hundred	Very few (perhaps only one) unless spent fuel is used

Source: CRS

Lessons

If an RDD attack occurred, the United States could draw many lessons from it.

- An attack could reveal failures of prevention. Did any intelligence failures result in not thwarting the attack, and what changes could be made? How was the material obtained (theft, insider assistance, poor security, etc.)? How did terrorists manage to avoid having it detected?

- An attack would test response capability. How quickly was federal aid brought to bear? How well were federal programs coordinated with each other and with state and local personnel? Did first responders have equipment and training needed for search and rescue? How quickly were emergency instructions broadcast, and how effective were they in stemming panic and saving lives? If instructions were given to shelter in place, how many people evacuated anyway, and did they interfere with the work of first responders? Were first responders from federal, state, and local agencies able to communicate, or did communication problems seen in other disasters remain unresolved? How quickly were decontamination facilities set up, and were there enough of them? Exercises may help prepare for an attack, but cannot provide high-confidence answers to these and other questions because they cannot mobilize a response involving thousands of people at all levels of government working under the chaos and pressure of a real-world situation.

- An attack would test recovery capability, such as decontamination techniques and disposal paths for contaminated materials.

- An attack would test whether nuclear, radiological, and conventional forensics techniques could determine where the material or weapon came from.

Difficult Metrics

It would be useful to know how much the United States spends on all aspects of countering RDDs, whether the probability of an RDD attack has increased or decreased, and what impact an RDD attack would have. Measuring these variables would help Congress make such spending decisions as whether to allocate more funds to: defense against RDDs or chemical weapons, intelligence or securing radioactive sources, or securing sources domestically or overseas. However, it appears that metrics for these variables are difficult if not impossible to obtain.

Budget

It would be exceedingly difficult, if not impossible, to determine how much money the federal government spends to prevent, respond to, and recover from an RDD attack. As noted throughout this report, many agencies have programs that deal with such an attack. A few programs are specific to RDDs. The FY2012 NNSA budget request includes $20.0 million for domestic radiological material removal and the same amount for international radiological material removal.[223] In other cases, RDD-related funds are not tracked separately. Some NRC programs support safety and security of radioactive sources, but the agency's budget does not break out funds directly relevant to RDDs, and the great majority of its budget is related to nuclear reactors, including reactor safety, fuel facilities, and storage, transport, and disposition of spent fuel.[224] Regarding DOD, GAO found that "although DOD compiles a biennial list of programs 'strongly related to combating WMD' and related costs, it cannot identify with precision what proportion of its resources are devoted specifically to counterproliferation."[225]

Further, almost all RDD-related spending is commingled with that of other programs in such categories as radiological and nuclear ("rad/nuke"), CBRN, WMD (weapons of mass destruction, often taken to mean CBRN), CBRNE (CBRN plus high-energy explosives), preparedness for and response to natural or accidental disasters, counterterrorism, and intelligence, and many programs that would address an RDD attack are byproducts of other programs. For example, equipment to detect terrorist nuclear weapons or material, such as that deployed by Customs and Border Protection, can detect many other types of radioactive material. Nuclear forensics, which for decades focused on analyzing samples of material from nuclear explosions, could help determine the source of materials from nuclear weapons and RDDs. Intelligence agencies focusing on nuclear weapons might detect an RDD plot. Many programs that would help respond to an RDD

---

[223] U.S. Department of Energy. *FY 2012 Congressional Budget Request,* volume 1, p. 421.

[224] U.S. Nuclear Regulatory Commission, *Congressional Budget Justification for FY 2011,* NUREG-1100, volume 26, February 2010, p. 3, http://www.nrc.gov/reading-rm/doc-collections/nuregs/staff/sr1100/v26/sr1100v26.pdf. According to NRC staff, "information pertaining to the amount of money spent each year to protect the U.S. against the threat of dirty bombs is not within the scope of the NRC's budget." Personal communication, July 30, 2010.

[225] U.S. Government Accountability Office, *Weapons of Mass Destruction: Actions Needed to Track Budget Execution for Counterproliferation Programs and Better Align Resources with Combating WMD Strategy,* GAO-10-755R, September 28, 2010, p. 3, http://www.gao.gov/new.items/d10755r.pdf.

attack were established to respond to such peacetime emergencies as a nuclear power plant accident, a train accident involving hazardous chemicals, or a hurricane. Such programs provide equipment and training for first responders, medical countermeasures, and evacuation plans. Separating out the RDD component from various federal programs would be difficult indeed. Doing the same for state and local efforts would be difficult as well.

Probability of an RDD Attack

U.S. ability to prevent, respond to, and recover from an RDD attack has improved greatly since 9/11, and continues to improve, because of the accretion of layer upon layer of capability in many areas. However, as with an arms race or sports, improvement by one side does not provide an advantage if the other side makes comparable, greater, or offsetting improvements. It thus seems hard to assess qualitatively if the United States is more secure against an RDD attack now than it was before 9/11. Determining the probability of an RDD attack or how it has changed since then would be harder because the data may be difficult to gather and inferences based on the data may be tenuous. For example: (1) The number of unsecured radioactive sources is related to the threat but may not be highly correlated to it. Terrorists need to steal only one Category 1 or 2 source to make one or more RDDs; it will be many years before every source is secured against insider and outsider threats. (2) Terrorist intent correlates with threat, but possible metrics of intent, such as communications about an RDD attack, would be hard to gather and might be deliberately misleading. (3) Terrorist acquisition of expertise to make an RDD may correlate with the threat, but it may take only one or a few people to provide that expertise, and determining whether a terrorist group has tapped into those people could be difficult. (4) Predictions about terrorist threats may look arbitrary or alarmist. For example, the Commission on the Prevention of WMD Proliferation and Terrorism opened its report by stating, "The Commission believes that unless the world community acts decisively and with great urgency, it is more likely than not that a weapon of mass destruction will be used in a terrorist attack somewhere in the world by the end of 2013." But might the probability be 25 percent? Might it be as high as 75 percent? Why 2013 instead of 2011 or 2020?

Even if intelligence agencies could generate the probability of an RDD attack, it is unclear if that information would be of use to Congress. If the probability dropped from 50 percent five years ago to 25 percent now, would Congress reduce the amount of funds dedicated to preventing, responding to, and recovering from an RDD attack by half? Probability would be but one of many factors affecting budget decisions. Further, an assessment that an RDD attack has become less likely over the past five years would not necessarily indicate the likelihood over the next five.

Impact of an Attack

Decisions on allocation of funds among various CBRN-related programs would benefit by knowing the value of such programs. One way to assess value would be to measure the impact of various CBRN attacks. For example, if an attack using one type of CBRN would have ten times the impact of another, it might be appropriate to spend ten times as much to counter the first attack as the second.

Measuring impact, however, is difficult. (1) Even lives lost, the most straightforward metric, is difficult to estimate. A scenario might generate an estimate of deaths resulting from an RDD attack, but the estimate would depend on the assumptions used to create the scenario. Estimating lives lost in chemical, biological, and nuclear attacks is more difficult because the plausible range of fatalities is greater. (2) Some might challenge a scenario on grounds that assumptions were selected to produce a desired result. (3) Impact may be out of proportion to lives lost. The anthrax attacks of 2001 killed "only" five people but resulted in a great many security measures that cost significant amounts of money. The attacks of 9/11 killed some 3,000 people and led to two wars that cost hundreds of billions of dollars and killed thousands of soldiers and civilians. (4) The political impact of deaths from an attack is greater than that of deaths from accidents. For comparison, 33,808 people were killed in U.S. traffic accidents in 2009, but the political response has been less than was the case for the 9/11 attacks. (5) Another metric of impact is cost. But cost hinges on assumptions, and cost estimates of an RDD attack vary widely. Would buildings be demolished, or could R&D provide means to decontaminate at lower cost? (6) Another impact of an RDD attack is the dose level to which key areas would have to be remediated, which would affect the restricted area, the time an area was restricted, and the cost of cleanup, yet it is not clear what dose the public would consider acceptable. (7) An RDD could have significant psychological and societal impacts that could be hard to anticipate, let alone to measure. Given public fear of radiation, an attack could shake people's sense of personal security and alter patterns of daily life.

Issues for Congress

This report shows that the United States and others have done much to prevent, respond to, and recover from an RDD attack, but that more might be done. In so doing, it raises many issues that Congress may wish to consider, notably the priority for countering radiological vs. other forms of terrorism and where resources for enhancing security against RDDs might most efficiently be deployed.

Priority for countering radiological terrorism: It is difficult to know what priority should be given to countering radiological terrorism as opposed to other forms of terrorism. Some arguments suggest that the United States should be doing more in this arena, while other arguments suggest doing less. (1) Despite concerns about terrorist interest in radiological material, there has been no successful RDD attack. (2) Of nuclear, chemical, biological, and radiological weapons, the latter would arguably kill the fewest people. (3) Radiological terrorism has arguably received less attention than other forms of CBRN terrorism. The April 2010 Nuclear Security Summit focused on nuclear terrorism. U.N. Security Council Resolution 1540 focused on nuclear, biological, and chemical weapons, though it also references security of radioactive sources. [226] (4) As noted under "Budget," most planning, training, equipment, and supplies that would help respond to an RDD attack would be of use in other disasters as well, whether natural, accidental, or terrorist in origin, so that it is difficult to determine the balance between funds to counter all hazards and those to counter RDDs only. (5) Since costs resulting from an RDD attack could be tens of billions of dollars, some measures that are directly relevant to an RDD attack, such as decontamination R&D and programs to secure radioactive sources, may be cost-effective.

Domestic vs. overseas expenditures to secure radioactive sources: Where are U.S. funds to secure radioactive sources most effectively spent? One argument is that it is better to spend money to secure domestic radiological sources because if they are illicitly obtained they could be used promptly in an RDD, avoiding the risk of detection in other countries and at U.S. ports of

---

[226] United Nations Security Council, *Resolution 1540*, S/Res/1540 (2004), April 28, 2004, p. 3, http://daccess-dds-ny.un.org/doc/UNDOC/GEN/N04/328/43/PDF/N0432843.pdf?OpenElement.

entry. This effort would be costly. Kenneth Luongo, president of Partnership for Global Security, pointed to one cost element. He urged that "all radiological sources in public buildings, beginning with metropolitan hospitals," should be secured, and estimates that it would cost about $125 million to complete such projects at all 500 U.S. metropolitan hospitals.[227] Of course, it would also be costly to secure radiological sources in countries that could not do so without international assistance. On the other hand, funds spent securing sources overseas might offer more leverage in that many sources overseas may have a lower level of security than do U.S. sources. Programs to secure sources in other nations could also promote a security culture, leveraging U.S. expenditures. A further consideration is that expenditures to counter the RDD threat overseas could help safeguard the many U.S. facilities in other nations, such as military bases and embassies, and could help avert RDD attacks on critical facilities, such as seaports, that could cause economic disruption.

Radiation detection networks: While attention has focused on explosive-driven "dirty bombs," an unobtrusive RDD attack could go undetected for hours, giving material time to spread and to irradiate people. A distributed network of sensors to detect, locate, and identify radioactive material would address this issue. Sensors could be mounted on buildings, police cars, or surveillance cameras. Work is underway to develop radiation-detection chips to be incorporated into cell phones or other mobile devices.[228] What would it cost to develop a detector network and deploy it in major metropolitan areas? Would it be appropriate for the federal government to fund deployment of such networks, or would deployment be a state or local responsibility?

Decontamination information and R&D: The main physical effect of an RDD would be contamination of high-value areas, and the main cost would be decontamination. Yet decontamination is complicated. The proper methods depend on the RDD material, its form, the types of surfaces on which it is deposited, and the required decontamination level. "First decontaminators" (as distinct from first responders, who would be focused on more immediate tasks) would presumably be less highly trained than experts from national laboratories and elsewhere. Yet they should be aware of what decontamination techniques would be ineffective or could worsen an RDD's effects. According to GAO,

> Lawrence Livermore National Laboratory decontamination experts told us that the conventional use of high-pressure hosing to decontaminate a building is effective under normal conditions but could be the wrong cleanup approach for an RDD using cesium-137. In this case, the imbibing (absorbing) properties of some porous surfaces such as concrete would actually cause this soluble radioactive isotope to penetrate even further into surfaces making subsequent decontamination more difficult and destructive.[229]

---

[227] Kenneth Luongo, *The 2010 Nuclear Security Summit: Seizing the Opportunity to Improve Global Nuclear Material Security and Prevent Nuclear Terrorism*, Partnership for Global Security, A briefing hosted by the National Security Network and Center for Arms Control and Non-Proliferation, April 7, 2010, http://www.partnershipforglobalsecurity.org/PDFFrameset.asp?PDF= luongo_nuclear_security_summit_hill_briefing.pdf.

[228] Benjamin Sutherland, "My Blackberry as a Bomb Sniffer?," *Newsweek*, September 27, 2008, http://www.newsweek.com/2008/09/26/my-blackberry-as-a-bomb-sniffer.print.html; Emil Venere and Elizabeth Gardner, "Cell Phone Sensors Detect Radiation to Thwart Nuclear Terrorism," Purdue University news release, January 22, 2008, http://news.uns.purdue.edu/x/2008a/080122FischbachNuclear.html; and personal communication, Simon Labov, Associate Program Leader for Detection Systems, Lawrence Livermore National Laboratory, February 14, 2011.

[229] U.S. Government Accountability Office, *Combating Nuclear Terrorism: Actions Needed to Better Prepare to Recover from Possible Attacks Using Radiological or Nuclear Materials*, GAO-10-204, January 2010, p. 16, (continued...)

Prompt availability of relevant information, such as through FEMA's Lessons Learned Information Sharing,[230] would help avoid such mistakes. Should this or other databases be augmented to include information for first decontaminators?

Preparing for decontamination: Some existing equipment can readily identify the material used in an RDD. That data, however, would be of little value for decontamination unless the proper equipment and supplies, and training for their use, were available. Cities, especially those that had not obtained such resources, would inevitably turn to the federal government for support following an attack. Has the government stockpiled the needed resources for decontamination or arranged to have it manufactured quickly in the quantities needed? To what extent is the stockpile updated in light of new R&D? What areas might future R&D pursue? Note that the capability to decontaminate areas struck in an RDD attack would also be of value for decontaminating the much larger area receiving radioactive fallout in the event of an IND attack.

Waste disposition and RDDs: Many studies, over decades, have considered how to dispose of nuclear waste. Since 1999, after decades of study and multiple lawsuits, defense waste has been buried at the Waste Isolation Pilot Plant (WIPP) in a salt bed in New Mexico.[231] The issue of a permanent repository for spent fuel from nuclear power plants has been studied, and unresolved, for decades. This issue is relevant to preventing an RDD attack because spent fuel could be used in an RDD. Political and technical considerations have blocked burial of such waste at Yucca Mountain, Nevada.[232] In 2010, the Secretary of Energy, at the direction of the President, established the Blue Ribbon Commission on America's Nuclear Future "to conduct a comprehensive review of policies for managing the back end of the nuclear fuel cycle."[233]

The possibility of an RDD attack adds urgency to the disposition of radioactive waste. Most sealed sources have no disposition pathway, so disused sources are stored in ways that are less secure than, for example, deep underground burial. Deciding on a pathway for permanent disposition of such sources—which would not occupy a large volume—would reduce the risk of terrorists obtaining material that could be used in an attack. On a vastly larger scale, if decontamination following an RDD attack proved ineffective, an alternative would be to demolish contaminated buildings and dig up streets, generating huge amounts of rubble. Where would it go? If buried, would it contaminate the water table? If it were to be buried out of state, would another state accept it? How would it be transported? Would it contaminate the route along which it traveled? Would states along the proposed route try to block transit? It is beyond the

---

(...continued)

http://www.gao.gov/new.items/d10204.pdf.

[230] U.S. Department of Homeland Security. Federal Emergency Management Agency. "Lessons Learned Information Sharing," https://www.llis.dhs.gov/index.do.

[231] For information on WIPP, see U.S. Department of Energy. "Waste Isolation Pilot Plant," http://www.wipp.energy.gov/. For further information on WIPP and the surrounding salt bed, see James Conca, Sondra Sage, and Judith Wright, "Nuclear Energy and Waste Disposal in the Age of Fuel Recycling," *New Mexico Journal of Science*, vol. 45 (December 2008), pp. 13-21, http://www.nmas.org/NMJoS-Volume-45.pdf.

[232] For a brief history of the Yucca Mountain project and an archive of articles from 1985 on, see "Yucca Mountain," *New York Times*, http://topics.nytimes.com/top/news/national/usstatesterritoriesandpossessions/nevada/yucca-mountain/index.html. For further information, see CRS Report RL33461, *Civilian Nuclear Waste Disposal*, by Mark Holt, and CRS Report R40202, *Nuclear Waste Disposal: Alternatives to Yucca Mountain*, by Mark Holt.

[233] U.S. Department of Energy. "Blue Ribbon Commission on America's Nuclear Future, U.S. Department of Energy: Advisory Committee Charter," filed March 1, 2010, http://www.brc.gov/pdfFiles/BRC_Charter.pdf. See also the commission's website, http://www.brc.gov/.

---

scope of this study to suggest alternatives, but it would appear to be more efficient to plan in advance how to dispose of this rubble rather than deciding on a rushed basis postattack.

Standards for background investigations: NRC's Increased Controls order requires employers to check the background of employees for trustworthiness and reliability to determine who can have unescorted access to Category 1 and 2 sources. While some radiation safety officers (RSOs) interviewed for this report saw this process as flawed and others did not, all agreed that there are no uniform standards for disqualification, and all treated as proprietary the standards they developed. Several looked for a pattern of behavior rather than specific disqualifying items. At some organizations, human resources personnel made the judgment as to whether an applicant was trustworthy and reliable; at others, the RSO made the call; at others, an in-house security expert did; and at still others, a committee did. All agreed it was considerably more difficult to evaluate a foreign national than a U.S. citizen. As a result, an individual might be granted unescorted access by one organization but not by another. Congress could address this issue in several ways:

- Decide that while the current approach to screening is inconsistently implemented, various organizations have been able to make it work, each in its own way, so that no action is called for.

- Each licensee with Category 1 or 2 sources has individuals charged with deciding whether applicants are trustworthy and reliable. Direct NRC, FBI, or another agency to train those individuals on how to examine personnel background information, what clues to look for, what factors are disqualifying, etc.

- Direct NRC to specify grounds for disqualification in its regulations, with a further requirement to refer hard-to-resolve cases to the FBI.

- For foreign nationals for whom a comprehensive background investigation cannot be performed in a reasonable time or expense, permit access to Category 1 and 2 sources only when escorted by an individual cleared for unescorted access.

Modify a materials-protection program: The GTRI Domestic Materials Protection Program visits facilities requesting the service, examines the security situation, and installs devices to enhance security. It provides this service on a voluntary basis at no initial cost to the facilities.[234] As of February 2011, this program had "identified more than 2,700 vulnerable buildings … with high-priority radioactive material in the United States" and had completed security enhancements at 251 of them "with the remainder aiming to be completed by 2025."[235] Other upgrades will take several years as well, as detailed in **Appendix B**. Congress could maintain the program at its current level. One alternative is to expand it, completing the upgrades sooner in an effort to reduce the risk that terrorists could seize radioactive material in the United States and quickly use it in an RDD. Other alternatives include eliminating the program or making it mandatory. According to an NRC-NNSA document, the NRC and state regulatory "framework provides a *common baseline level of security to ensure adequate protection* of public health and safety and the common defense and security." Further, NNSA *"build[s] on the existing regulatory requirements by providing voluntary security enhancements"* that "are *complementary to and do*

---

[234] As noted earlier, GTRI installs security upgrades and provides initial maintenance, while the facility must agree to provide all further maintenance.

[235] U.S. Department of Energy. National Nuclear Security Administration. "NNSA: Securing Domestic Radioactive Material," fact sheet, February 1, 2011, p. 2.

not replace the licensees obligation to meet NRC and Agreement State regulatory requirements."[236] If these requirements are sufficient, are the GTRI enhancements needed? If they are not sufficient, why are the enhancements voluntary and who should bear their cost?

Radiological forensics: Congress has given nuclear forensics overwhelming support. For example, the Nuclear Forensics and Attribution Act (H.R. 730; P.L. 111-140, Feb. 16, 2010) passed the House, 402-16, and the Senate by unanimous consent. It focused on radiological as well as nuclear weapons and materials. Given this congressional support, options likely to be of interest to Congress involve how to strengthen radiological forensics capability, not whether to do so. Options include:

- Recognize that nuclear forensics and radiological forensics have important differences. This is the basis for addressing radiological forensic measures separately.

- Require a report. Radiological forensics is typically grouped together with nuclear forensics and rarely considered separately. To examine its unique aspects and requirements, Congress could direct the Department of Energy or DNDO's National Technical Nuclear Forensics Center to task an outside panel to conduct a study on this topic and how its science and technology might be advanced.

- Support the buildout of archives of physical samples relevant to RDDs. In the course of CRS discussions with multiple government agencies, experts who were in a position to know said that their agencies did not have an archive of sealed sources or of radioactive materials that might be of interest for an RDD. Such archives would be valuable for matching RDD debris against samples and would provide an investigation with other clues as well. It would be important to maintain archives on an ongoing bases, as designs, manufacturing processes, and materials change over time.

- Consider mandating U.S. producers of radioactive material and sealed sources to include trace amounts of impurities, differing from one batch to the next, to distinguish between batches of materials. When matched with records of sales, these "fingerprints" would provide clues to the provenance of the items. Consider requesting other countries to direct their producers to do likewise.

- Maintain liaison with manufacturers of radioactive materials and sealed sources to expedite communication between them and the government in the event of an RDD attack.

Legislation

Several bills enacted into law in the 111th Congress dealt with radiological terrorism:

H.R. 2647 (P.L. 111-84), FY2010 National Defense Authorization Act (Skelton). Section 1036 called for the President to develop a five-year plan for improving U.S. nuclear forensic and attribution capabilities, including recommendations with respect to "methods for the attribution of

---

[236] U.S. Nuclear Regulatory Commission and National Nuclear Security Administration, *Partnership for Securing Nuclear and Radioactive Materials*, March 31, 2010, pp. 1-2, original emphasis, http://www.doh.state.fl.us/ environment/radiation/radmat/NRC-Items/sp10029.pdf.

nuclear or radiological material to the source when such material is intercepted by the United States, foreign governments, or international bodies or is dispersed in the course of a terrorist attack or other nuclear or radiological explosion." The bill was signed into law October 28, 2009.

H.R. 730 (P.L. 111-140), Nuclear Forensics and Attribution Act (Schiff), sought to augment U.S. capability to identify the source of nuclear and other radioactive material used in a terrorist attack by establishing the National Technical Nuclear Forensics Center (NTNFC) within the Domestic Nuclear Detection Office of the Department of Homeland Security. This center would coordinate U.S. capability to conduct forensics analysis. The act also provided for scholarships, fellowships, and grants to develop expertise in this area. The bill was signed into law February 16, 2010.

H.R. 2701 (P.L. 111-259), FY2010 Intelligence Authorization Act (Reyes). Section 344 provided, "Not later than 180 days after the date of the enactment of this Act, the Director of National Intelligence, in consultation with the Nuclear Regulatory Commission, shall submit to Congress a report summarizing intelligence related to the threat to the United States from weapons that use radiological materials, including highly dispersible substances such as cesium-137." The bill was signed into law on October 7, 2010.

Several bills in the 112th Congress deal with radiological terrorism:

S. 860 (Levin). The bill would "ensure that methodologies and technologies used by the Bureau of Customs and Border Protection to screen for and detect the presence of chemical, nuclear, biological, and radiological weapons in municipal solid waste are as effective as the methodologies and technologies used by the Bureau to screen for those materials in other items of commerce entering the United States through commercial motor vehicle transport." Introduced April 14, 2011 and referred to the Committee on Homeland Security and Governmental Affairs.

H.R. 1411 (Bilirakis), Metropolitan Medical Response System Program Act of 2011. The bill would, among other things, provide grants "to strengthen chemical, biological, radiological , nuclear, and explosive detection, response, and decontamination capabilities." Introduced April 7, 2011, and referred to the Committee on Energy and Commerce.

Appendix A. Technical Background

This Appendix presents technical aspects connected with RDDs. It offers a stand-alone tutorial for those desiring a more in-depth treatment of this subject. In expanding on the material in the main text, this Appendix repeats some of the material presented there.

Radiation

Atoms have a nucleus that is surrounded by electrons. The nucleus is made up of protons, which have a positive electrical charge, and (with one exception) neutrons, which have no charge. Electrons have a negative charge. Atoms typically have an equal number of protons and electrons, and are thus electrically neutral. Isotopes are forms of a chemical element with the same number of electrons and protons but different numbers of neutrons. For example, all three isotopes of hydrogen have one proton and one electron, but the most common form of hydrogen has no neutrons, while deuterium has one neutron and tritium has two.

Most atoms that make up the Earth's crust are stable: they will remain in their current form indefinitely. Each chemical element, however, has one or more unstable isotopes. These elements disintegrate or "decay," usually transforming into an atom of a different element.[237] Atoms that decay are "radioactive," radioactive atoms are called "radionuclides." Decay is typically accompanied by emission of particles, and often photons as well; such emissions are called radiation. "Radionuclide" refers to the properties of atoms, such as the types and energies of particles given off by decay, while "radioactive material" refers to bulk properties of radionuclides, such as the amount that would contaminate a certain area. Rate of decay is measured in units of curies (Ci), where $1 \text{ Ci} = 3.7 \times 10^{10}$ disintegrations per second.[238] A related measure, specific activity, counts disintegrations per gram of material per second, e.g., in curies per gram; the higher the specific activity, the more disintegrations there are per gram of material per second. Specific activity permits comparison of the radioactivity of different materials. Curies and specific activity measure number of disintegrations, not their energy. A related measure is the half-life, the time for half the atoms of a radioactive material to decay.

Radiation takes several main forms.

- Alpha particles (two protons and two neutrons): Because they are massive by subatomic standards, alpha particles must carry off a considerable amount of energy to escape the nucleus; at the same time, because of their mass they can travel only an inch in air. They are stopped by a sheet of paper or the dead outer layers of skin.

- Beta particles (an electron or a positron, the latter being a positively-charged electron): These are much less massive than alpha particles, so they can travel up to several feet in air, but are less energetic than alpha particles. Some are stopped by outer layers of skin, while others can penetrate a few millimeters.

---

[237] Another mode of decay in which an atom emits a photon but remains the same chemical element is not relevant to this report.

[238] The International System of Units uses the becquerel (Bq), which is one disintegration per second, instead of the curie. This report uses curies because this unit is more widely used in the United States.

- Neutrons. Some radionuclides decay by emitting a neutron. Neutrons are lighter than alpha particles but much heavier than beta particles. They can travel tens of meters in air. Neutrons are also emitted when atoms of heavier elements fission, or split into two or more pieces; fission also releases large quantities of energy. Neutrons are typically stopped by hydrogen-containing material, such as water or plastic. Energetic neutrons can penetrate the body.

- Gamma rays: These are photons released during radioactive decay. Photons may be thought of as packets of electromagnetic energy (discussed next), and have no rest mass. Gamma rays have a wide range of energies; more energetic ones can travel hundreds of meters in air. They can be stopped by dense material like lead.

The electromagnetic spectrum includes the entire range of electromagnetic energy, such as, in order of increasing energy, radio waves, infrared, visible light, ultraviolet, and x-rays and gamma rays.[239] Photons transmit electromagnetic energy; a photon's energy determines whether it is, say, a radio wave or visible light. Gamma rays have a range of energies, but those from materials that might be used for RDDs have medium to high energies and can penetrate the human body, causing biological damage. The higher the energy, the more material they can penetrate and the greater the damage. Gamma ray energy is measured in electron volts or, more commonly, thousands of electron volts, abbreviated keV.[240] Different materials emit gamma rays at different energies. **Figure A-1** plots the number of gamma rays counted in 5 minutes (vertical axis) against their energies (horizontal axis). It shows that cobalt-60 emits two main gamma rays when it decays, at 1,173 keV and 1,333 keV, while cesium-137 emits (through an intermediate step)[241] mainly gamma rays at 662 keV. Each radionuclide emits its own unique gamma-ray spectrum when it decays, as exemplified by **Figure A-1**, a characteristic of great use for identifying radionuclides.

Each radionuclide decays in a specific way. Strontium-90 emits beta particles when it decays, but not gamma rays.[242] Cobalt-60 emits high-energy gamma rays, making it readily detectable; it also emits beta particles. Americium-241 decays by emitting alpha particles, and also emits some gamma rays, mainly of low energy.

---

[239] For an introduction to the electromagnetic spectrum, see U.S. National Aeronautics and Space Administration, "Electromagnetic Spectrum," http://imagine.gsfc nasa.gov/docs/science/know_11/emspectrum html. For a graphic of the electromagnetic spectrum, see Lawrence Berkeley National Laboratory, "The Electromagnetic Spectrum," http://www.lbl.gov/MicroWorlds/ALSTool/EMSpec/EMSpec2.html.

[240] "An electron volt is a measure of energy. An electron volt is the kinetic energy gained by an electron passing through a potential difference of one volt." Fermi National Accelerator Laboratory, "How Big Is an Electron Volt?," http://www-bd.fnal.gov/public/electronvolt html.

[241] "The radionuclide cesium-137 … has a 30.17-year half-life and decays by beta decay to barium-137, which is stable, in 15 percent of the decays and to barium-137m, a metastable radionuclide, in 85 percent of the decays. Barium-137m decays to stable barium-137 with a half-life of 2.55 minutes, emitting a 661.7 keV gamma ray." National Research Council. Division on Earth and Life Studies. Nuclear and Radiation Studies Board. Committee on Radiation Source Use and Replacement, *Radiation Source Use and Replacement, Abbreviated Version*, Washington, DC, 2008, p. 27, http://www nap.edu/catalog.php?record_id=11976.

[242] U.S. Environmental Protection Agency. "Radiation Protection: Strontium," http://www.epa.gov/radiation/radionuclides/strontium html.

Biological Effects of Ionizing Radiation[243]

Understanding an RDD's potential effectiveness—whether in terms of biological damage, area denial, or as a weapon of terror—requires understanding the physiological effects of radiation. Radiation strikes people constantly, but most of it, like radio waves and light, is not "ionizing." Ionizing radiation has enough energy to knock electrons out of atoms, creating electrically-charged particles called ions that can damage cells.[244] "[O]nly a very small amount of energy needs to be deposited in a cell or tissue to produce significant biological change."[245] There is a very low risk of effects at very low doses of radiation, but higher doses may lead to cancer, genetic mutations, sickness, or death. Effects may be of two types. "Deterministic effects are those for which the severity of the effect varies with the dose, and for which a threshold may therefore occur. Stochastic effects are those for which the probability that an effect will occur, rather than the severity of the effect, is regarded as a function of the dose, without threshold."[246] Deterministic effects include nausea, vomiting, diarrhea, hemorrhage, and, at high doses delivered in a short time over the whole body, death within hours to weeks; stochastic effects include cancers and genetic damage.[247] Contamination from an RDD is unlikely to produce deterministic effects in many people. The concern is that residual contamination may produce stochastic effects, so that some (if not many) people will not want to reoccupy the area.

---

[243] For further information on this topic, see Dade Moeller, *Environmental Health,* revised edition (Cambridge, Harvard University Press, 1997); U.S. Department of Health and Human Services, "Radiation Emergency Medical Management," http://www remm nlm.gov/; and U.S. Uniformed Services University of the Health Sciences. Armed Forces Radiobiology Research Institute. "Emergency Response Resources," http://www.afrri.usuhs mil/outreach/emergency_response.html.

[244] For information on how ionizing radiation affects cells, see Princeton University, "Open Source Radiation Safety Training: Module 3: Biological Effects," http://web.princeton.edu/sites/ehs/osradtraining/biologicaleffects/page htm#Mechanisms.

[245] Moeller, *Environmental Health,* p. 247.

[246] Ibid., p. 248.

[247] Ibid., p. 250-251, and information provided by William Rhodes, Sandia National Laboratory, personal communication, December 17, 2010..

Figure A-1. Gamma-Ray Spectra of Cobalt-60 and Cesium-137

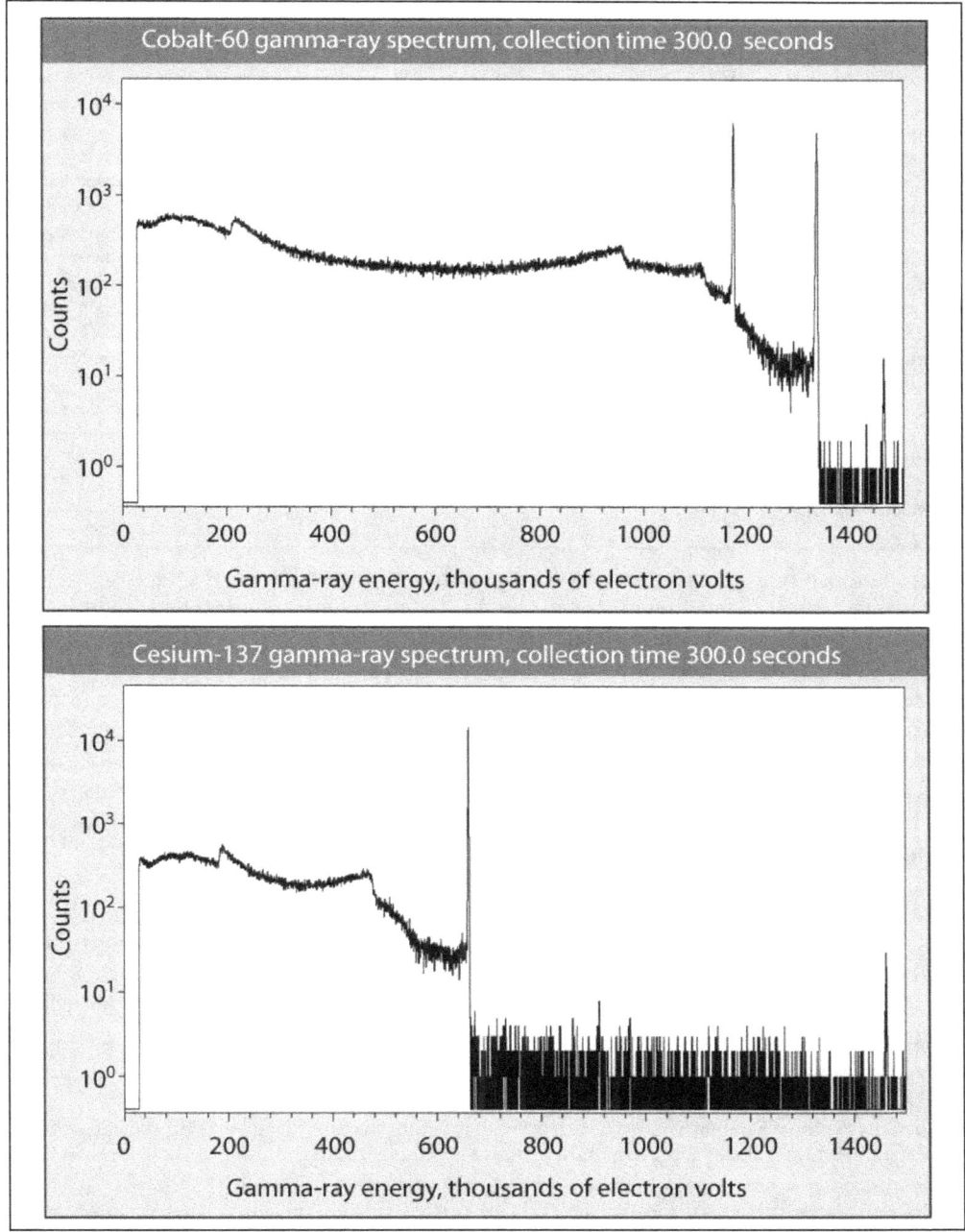

Source: Prepared by Scott Garner, Technical Staff Member, Los Alamos National Laboratory, September 2010.

Notes: This figure shows simulated gamma-ray spectra for cobalt-60 (top) and cesium-137 as they would be collected in 5 minutes by a high-resolution detector. In each spectrum, the x-axis indicates gamma-ray energy in thousands of electron volts (keV), and the y-axis, which uses a logarithmic scale, indicates number of counts (gamma rays) at each energy. The figure shows one peak for cesium-137 (via an intermediate step) at 662 keV, and two peaks for cobalt-60, at 1,173 and 1,333 keV. The top spectrum is for an unshielded 100-microcurie (0.089 microgram) source that would produce a dose of 0.55 millirem per hour at 50 cm from the source, while the bottom spectrum is for an unshielded 100-microcurie (1.2 microgram) source that would produce a dose of 0.15 millirem per hour at 50 cm from the source. "Biological Effects of Ionizing Radiation" discusses dose.

Is There a Minimum Threshold for Biological Effects of Radiation?

Low doses of radiation do not produce deterministic effects. A widely accepted view is that radiation below the threshold for such effects produces stochastic effects even at low doses. This view is called "linear, no threshold" because it extrapolates downward from higher doses that produce deterministic effects on the assumptions that (1) lower doses produce stochastic effects, and (2) there is no threshold below which effects do not occur. Another view is that there are no effects below some threshold. A Nuclear Regulatory Commission fact sheet presents both views: "The associations between radiation exposure and the development of cancer are mostly based on populations exposed to relatively high levels of ionizing radiation (e.g., Japanese atomic bomb survivors, and recipients of selected diagnostic or therapeutic medical procedures). ... Although radiation may cause cancer at high doses and high dose rates, there are no data to unequivocally establish the occurrence of cancer following exposure to low doses and low dose rates—below about [10 rem]. Those people living in areas having high levels of background radiation—above [1 rem] per year—such as Denver, Colorado have shown no adverse biological effects. Even so, the radiation protection community conservatively assumes that any amount of radiation may pose some risk for causing cancer and hereditary effect, and that the risk is higher for higher radiation exposures. A linear, no-threshold (LNT) dose response relationship is used to describe the relationship between radiation dose and the occurrence of cancer. This dose-response model suggests that any increase in dose, no matter how small, results in an incremental increase in risk. The LNT hypothesis is accepted by the NRC as a conservative model for determining radiation dose standards recognizing that the model may over estimate radiation risk." (U.S. Nuclear Regulatory Commission. "Fact Sheet on Biological Effects of Radiation," http://www.nrc.gov/reading-rm/doc-collections/fact-sheets/bio-effects-radiation.html. See also U.S. General Accounting Office. *Radiation Standards: Scientific Basis Inconclusive, and EPA and NRC Disagreement Continues.* RCED-00-152 June 30, 2000.)

While there is much public fear of any level of radiation, the physiological effects of an RDD, as well as the requirements for cleanup, depend on dose. Certain concepts and their units of measure are needed to discuss dose.[248] The roentgen (R) measures how much ionization a gamma ray produces when traveling through air.[249] The rad, for radiation absorbed dose, is used to correct a roentgen value for the amount of energy deposited into a substance, such as wood or human tissue. Another measure, the rem, or roentgen equivalent man, weights the cancer risk from different types of radiation deposited in human tissue. One rad of absorbed dose from x-rays, gamma rays, and beta particles is 1 rem. Because alpha particles and neutrons are much more massive, 1 rad of absorbed dose from them is much more harmful, so the weighting factor is 10 for neutrons and 20 for alpha particles.[250][251]

People are exposed to background levels of ionizing radiation every day from such sources as dirt and granite (which often contain traces of uranium, radium, and radioactive potassium), radon gas, and cosmic rays. Food and drinking water generally contain trace amounts of radioactive materials. The radiation dose from a jet airplane flight is 0.5 millirems (mrem) per hour in the air; from a chest x-ray, 6 mrem; and from living at an altitude of one mile, about 50 mrem/year.[252] A

---

[248] The rest of this paragraph is based on Moeller, *Environmental Health*, pp. 249-250.

[249] When a gamma ray travels through air, it pulls electrons away from atoms, leaving ions. The roentgen is defined only for gamma rays in air, not for other forms of radiation or other substances.

[250] The International System of Units uses different terms. For example, the gray (Gy) is 100 rad, and the sievert (Sv) is 100 rem. This report mostly uses roentgen, rad, and rem because they are more widely used in the United States.

[251] "The rad and rem are used to assess different aspects of the biological effects of radiation exposure. The absorbed dose (in units of rad) is generally used to evaluate the biological effects from short exposure times and relatively high levels of exposure. These types of biological effects (e.g., skin burns) have a threshold dose level, and the severity of the effect increases with the dose. The equivalent dose (in units of rem) is used to evaluate biological effects from long exposure times and relatively low levels of exposure. These probability of these effects in an exposed person (e.g., cancer) increases with dose, but the severity is independent of the dose received." Information provided by William Rhodes, Sandia National Laboratories, January 5, 2011.

[252] American Nuclear Society. "Radiation Dose Chart," http://www.ans.org/pi/resources/dosechart/. This interactive chart permits the user to adjust values to find an approximation of his or her total annual dose. One millirem is one thousandth of a rem.

2009 report shows an average annual dose of 620 mrem for the U.S. population, of which 48 percent (298 mrem) is from exposure to radiation for medical purposes.[253]

An RDD attack is likely to expose few people to a dose of more than a few rem per year, even using the unrealistic assumption that they remain in the affected area without sheltering for a year. Any effects from a dose of a few rem per year are likely to be stochastic. Views differ on the harm from that dose (see sidebar). Further, various standards imply different degrees of harm from a dose of a few rem per year. For dose to the public resulting from the nuclear fuel cycle (e.g., nuclear power plants), the Environmental Protection Agency (EPA) uses a standard of 25 mrem per year of whole-body dose.[254] NRC adopts that standard,[255] and in addition has a dose standard of 100 mrem per year for members of the public from operations licensed by NRC.[256] That agency also has established an occupational dose limit of 5 rem per year.[257] The occupational dose limit in Japan was reportedly 10 rem per year, a figure raised to 25 rem per year in the wake of the Fukushima Daiichi incident.[258] According to one expert, doses greater than 25 rem are often received in a short period of time, producing deterministic effects, the severity of which increases with dose.[259]

Exposure to radiation from an RDD can occur through four pathways. EPA lists three: direct, from sources external to the body; inhalation, breathing in particles of radioactive material; and ingestion, such as drinking water or eating food that contains radioactive material.[260] A fourth is through the skin. According to William Rhodes III, Senior Manager, International Security Systems Group, Sandia National Laboratories, "Skin is a very good barrier against many chemicals. However, certain radioactive chemicals, such as various compounds of tritium or iodine, can penetrate through intact skin and be taken up by the bloodstream and distributed throughout the body. Radioactive materials can also enter through the skin through wounds."[261] **Figure A-2** illustrates some of these pathways. Total dose is a combination of internal and external dose. The former is that portion of dose from radiation sources inside the body, while the latter is the portion from outside the body.

---

[253] National Council on Radiation Protection and Measurement, *Ionizing Radiation Exposure of the Population of the United States,* report 160 (2009), available through http://www ncrppublications.org/Reports/160. The figure of 620 mrem (6.2 millisievert) is from the council's webpage "NCRP Report No. 160 Section 1 Pie Chart," http://www.ncrponline.org/Publications/160_Pie_charts-Sec1.html, and the pie chart showing the contribution of various sources of radiation to dose is at http://www.ncrponline.org/images/160_pie_charts/Fig1-1.pdf.

[254] 10 CFR 190.10(a).

[255] 20 CFR 1301(e).

[256] 20 CFR 1301(a)(1).

[257] 20 CFR 1201(a)(1)(i).

[258] Keith Bradsher and Hiroko Tabuchi, "Last Defense at Troubled Reactors: 50 Japanese Workers," *New York Times,* March 16, 2011, p. 1.

[259] Dade Moeller, *Environmental Health,* revised edition (Cambridge, Harvard University Press, 1997), p. 250.

[260] For further information, see U.S. Environmental Protection Agency, "Radiation Protection: Exposure Pathways," http://www.epa.gov/radiation/understand/pathways html.

[261] Personal communications, June 7 and December 17, 2010.

Figure A-2. Radiation Exposure Pathways from an RDD

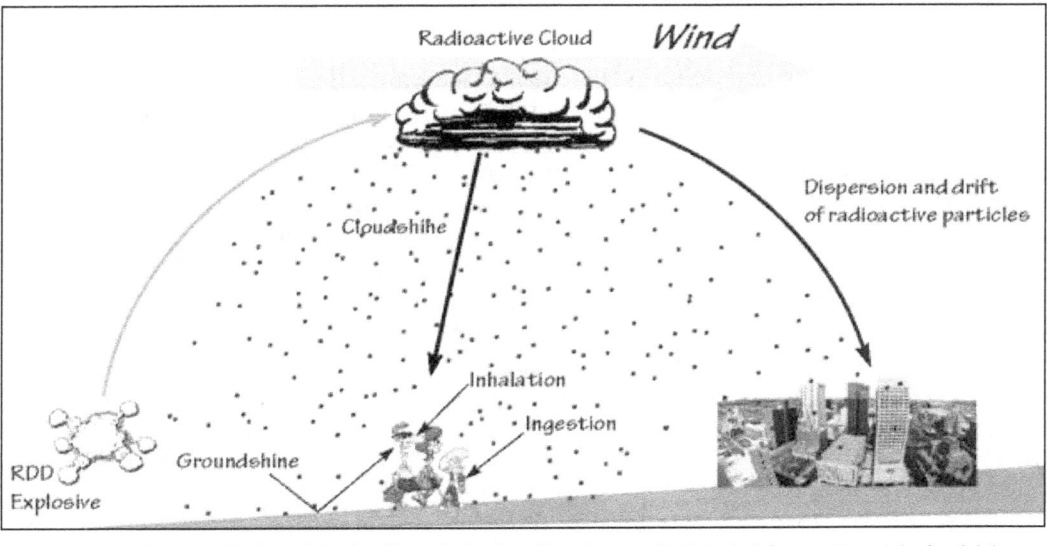

Source: Len Connell, William Rhodes III, and Heather Pennington, *Radiological Source Materials: Availability and Characteristics,* Sandia National Laboratories, SANDOC 2010-1184P, 2010.

Nuclear weapons generate massive amounts of radiation, both as prompt neutrons, gamma rays, x-rays, light, infrared, etc., near the explosion, and as gamma rays and other forms of radiation emitted by fallout over a wide area. The resulting doses can cause sickness or death in hours to months. RDDs do not involve a nuclear explosion and might contain some tens of grams of radioactive material, enough to contaminate several square miles, though many factors influence the effectiveness of an attack, as discussed under "Value of RDDs for Terrorists." As such, an RDD would generate a hazardous dose of radiation over a much smaller area than would a nuclear weapon.

In the affected area, an RDD attack would elevate the radiation level, and thus the dose, beyond background. EPA issued guidance in 1991 for protective actions following nuclear and radiological incidents except nuclear war, and the Federal Emergency Management Agency (FEMA) issued guidance in 2008 for protection and recovery following RDD and improvised nuclear device (IND, i.e., a terrorist-made nuclear weapon) incidents.[262][263] Both agencies recommended "protective action guides" (PAGs). A PAG is "the projected dose to a reference individual, from an accidental or deliberate release of radioactive material, at which a specific protective action to reduce or avoid that dose is recommended. Thus, protective actions are designed to be taken before the anticipated dose is realized."[264] The dose is that resulting from all

---

[262] U.S. Environmental Protection Agency. Office of Radiation Programs. *Manual of Protective Action Guides and Protective Actions for Nuclear Incidents,* revised 1991 (second printing, May 1992), http://www.epa.gov/radiation/docs/er/400-r-92-001.pdf; and Federal Emergency Management Agency, "Planning Guidance for Protection and Recovery Following Radiological Dispersal Device (RDD) and Improvised Nuclear Device (IND) Incidents," 73 *Federal Register* 45029-45048, August 1, 2008.

[263] The U.S. Centers for Disease Control and Prevention offers a guide to personal protection in the event of an RDD attack, "Frequently Asked Questions (FAQs) About Dirty Bombs," http://emergency.cdc.gov/radiation/dirtybombs.asp.

[264] Federal Emergency Management Agency, "Planning Guidance for Protection and Recovery Following Radiological Dispersal Device (RDD) and Improvised Nuclear Device (IND) Incidents," 73 *Federal Register*, August 1, 2008, p. 45034.

pathways, not just external sources. PAGs use predicted dose rates to provide guidance on emergency actions like sheltering in place or evacuation.

FEMA divides the incident response into three phases. The early phase starts "at the beginning of the incident when immediate decisions for effective protective actions are required, and when actual field measurement data generally are not available." The beginning is not necessarily clear. While an explosive-driven dirty bomb would announce its presence, FEMA observes that "in the event of a covert dispersal, discovery or detection may not occur for days or weeks."[265] For the early phase, for a PAG of 1 to 5 rem, the protective action recommendation is sheltering in place or evacuation.[266] The intermediate phase may follow in as little as a few hours. It "is usually assumed to begin after the incident source and releases have been brought under control and protective action decisions can be made based on measurements of exposure and radioactive materials that have been deposited."[267] For that phase, FEMA recommends "relocation of the public" for a projected dose of 2 rem for the first year and 0.5 rem per year for any subsequent year.[268][269] PAGs assume that a person is in the affected area, unprotected, 24 hours a day, 7 days a week, for the entire period. This is unrealistic; EPA expects, in the event of a nuclear reactor accident, that sheltering, radioactive decay, weathering, and simple decontamination techniques should reduce the actual dose in the 2-rem area to "less than one rem."[270] The late phase starts when recovery and cleanup begin, and ends when such actions have been completed.

An interagency group determined that the EPA PAGs for the early and intermediate phases were appropriate for use in an attack using an RDD or an improvised nuclear device (IND, a terrorist-made nuclear weapon).[271] EPA includes as "an objective of these PAGs to assure that ... the cumulative dose over 50 years (including the first and second years) will not exceed 5 rem."[272] FEMA does not include a PAG for the late phase because it would not be an emergency situation and because authorities would need to optimize among many factors (economic, land use, technical feasibility, etc.) in determining which areas need to be remediated to what levels.[273]

Another set of guidelines for emergency workers in the early phase covers doses at and above 5 rem, depending on the activity performed. The condition for exposure resulting in a 5-rem dose is that "all reasonably achievable actions have been taken to minimize dose." The activity that may warrant a 10-rem dose is "protecting valuable property necessary for public welfare (*e.g.,* a power plant)," and for a 25-rem dose, "lifesaving or protection of large populations. It is highly unlikely that doses would reach this level in an RDD incident." The conditions for exposure at both these levels are that the dose is unavoidable, responders are fully informed of risks, exposure is on a voluntary basis, appropriate personal protection like respirators is provided and used, and dose

---

[265] Ibid., p. 45032.

[266] Ibid., pp. 45032, 45035.

[267] Ibid., p. 45032.

[268] Ibid., p. 45035.

[269] The levels selected for PAGs were controversial. Some felt that PAG dose levels could be applied to situations other than a nuclear or RDD attack, supplanting standards that set dose at lower levels, which "could lead to dramatically weakened public protections." Douglas Guarino, "Obama Team to Review Contentious Bush EPA Nuclear Emergency Guide," *InsideEPA.com,* January 26, 2009.

[270] Environmental Protection Agency, *Manual of Protective Action Guides ...,* page 4-5.

[271] Ibid.

[272] Ibid., page 4-4.

[273] Federal Emergency Management Agency. "Planning Guidance for Protection and Recovery," pp. 45036-45037.

monitoring is available.[274] As noted earlier, even at the 25-rem level, there are "no detectable clinical effects [and a] small increase in the risk of delayed cancer and genetic effects.". However, the guidance states that "it is impossible to develop a single turn-back dose level for all responders to use in all events, especially those that involve lifesaving operations."[275]

A small amount of certain radioactive materials, if effectively dispersed, could contaminate a large area. If the bottle in **Figure A-3** contained radioactive cesium-137 chloride instead of nonradioactive cesium-133 chloride, it would have about 1,000 curies. If the vial in **Figure A-4** held pellets of radioactive cobalt-60 instead of nonradioactive cobalt-59, its curie count would be similar. Even this small amount of material can contaminate a substantial area to a high enough level to pose a threat to health. **Figure A-5** illustrates the point; it models a possible RDD attack on Washington, DC, using 1,000 curies of cesium-137 chloride.

Biological effects of radioactive material in an RDD depend on several factors in addition to dose.

- Type of radiation. Gamma emitters are the main source of direct exposure to radiation. Materials often mentioned as "candidates" for RDDs, like cobalt-60 and cesium-137, pose a threat mainly because even a fraction of a gram emits a huge number of high-energy gamma rays; such material is harmful whether outside or inside the body. Neutrons are also harmful whether inside or outside the body. An americium-beryllium mixture, used in oil well logging devices, is a neutron-emitting material in industrial use. In contrast, alpha emitters like americium-241 and polonium-210 are generally not harmful outside the body but are very harmful when taken into the body, where their energy is absorbed by live internal tissue.

---

[274] Federal Emergency Management Agency. "Planning Guidance for Protection and Recovery," p. 45037.
[275] Ibid.

Figure A-3. Cesium Chloride

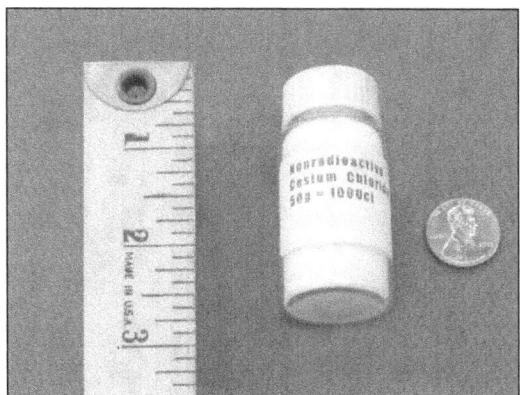

Source: Photo by CRS. Sample provided by National Nuclear Security Administration.

Notes: The bottle contains cesium-133 chloride, which is stable (non-radioactive). If the bottle held radioactive cesium-137 chloride, the 50 grams of material would contain about 1,000 curies.

Figure A-4. Cobalt

Source: Provided by National Nuclear Security Administration, July 2010.

Notes: The pellets are non-radioactive cobalt-59. Irradiating them in a nuclear reactor would convert them to radioactive cobalt-60. Their radioactivity would depend mainly on how long they remained in a reactor. Cobalt-60 pellets of this size typically contain 3 to 8 curies.

- Type of radionuclide. Different nuclides (radioactive or otherwise) behave differently in the body. Iodine concentrates in the thyroid gland. According to EPA, "Strontium-90 is chemically similar to calcium, and tends to deposit in bone and blood-forming tissue (bone marrow)."[276] Polonium does not concentrate in an organ but circulates throughout the body.

- Physical and chemical characteristics. Is the material in metallic, ceramic, or granular form? Is it soluble in water? Is it a pure element with one set of properties, or part of a chemical compound with different properties?

- Sources of long-term exposure. Some RDD materials would retain much of their radioactivity for years. Material remaining after cleanup, especially gamma emitters, would increase dose to people in the affected area. Filtering might not remove radioactive material from drinking water. Plants grown on contaminated land might take up radioactive material, and cattle eating contaminated plants might retain such material. Ingesting food or water with radioactive material would increase dose.

---

[276] U.S. Environmental Protection Agency. "Radiation Protection: Strontium." http://www.epa.gov/rpdweb00/radionuclides/strontium html#inbody.

Figure A-5. A Possible RDD Attack on Washington, DC
Using 1,000 Curies of Cesium-137 Chloride

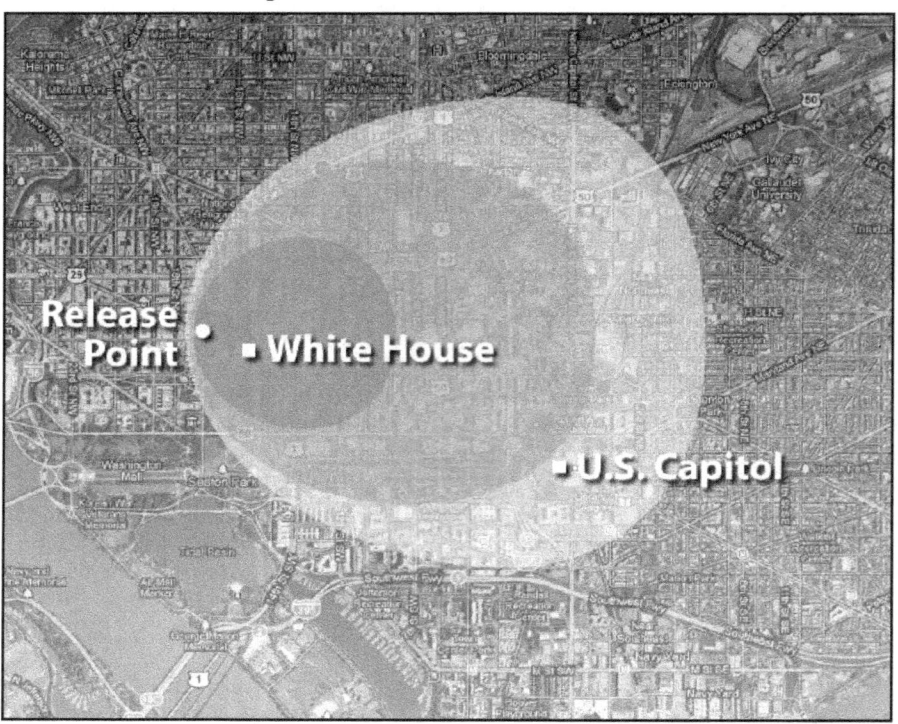

	Area km² mi²	Equivalent Dose (rem)	Exceeds relocation PAG for which year:	Population	All Cancers	Fatal Cancers
Effects and Actions						
	2.10 0.81	>2.00	First year only	38,000	233	159
	7.60 2.93	>0.500	Any subsequent year	94,700	278	189
	13.2 5.10	>5.00	50 years (cumulative)	125,000	461	314
Areas and counts are cumulative. RDD detonated at 38.9 N, 77.0 W. PAG: Protective Action Guide						

Source: William Rhodes III, Senior Manager, International Security Systems Group, Sandia National Laboratories, September 2010; analysis by Heather Pennington; graphics by Mona Aragon.

Note (provided by William Rhodes): This map, based on an atmospheric dispersion model, shows where individuals are projected to have an increased risk of developing cancers due to radiation exposure over a year or more. The RDD in this scenario uses 1,000 curies of cesium-137 chloride (about 50 grams). The model assumes that all material used is dispersed, but that it is not dispersed evenly over the area. Wind is assumed to be from west to east at 7 mph. The model includes exposure from radioactive material both deposited on the surface and resuspended into the air and inhaled. EPA and FEMA have developed Protective Action Guides (PAGs) to indicate when long-term relocation of individuals should be considered. PAGs are primarily based on an assessment of the risk of developing cancer over an exposed individual's lifetime. They assume, conservatively, that individuals are unsheltered and remain in the area during the entire period described for each contour. Contours show where individuals, if not relocated per the PAG, are projected to receive at least a specified dose in a specified time, as follows: inner contour (red), dose in first year post-attack, >2.00 rem; middle contour (orange), dose in second year post-attack, >0.500 rem; and outer contour (yellow), cumulative dose in the first 50 years post-attack, >5.00 rem. The cigar-shaped plumes often seen in models of atmospheric dispersion occur for gases or very fine particles, which would be the case for chemical warfare agents or fallout from a nuclear weapon but not in the case depicted. Whether such plumes would occur for an RDD depends on such factors as wind speed, type of explosive, and particle size.

(Provided by CRS): This note compares lifetime incidence of, and deaths from, cancer to those resulting from the attack modeled in this Figure. For the United States, the lifetime risk of being diagnosed with cancer is 43.61 percent, and the lifetime risk of dying from cancer is 21.15 percent. (U.S. National Institutes of Health. National Cancer Institute. Surveillance Epidemiology and End Results (SEER). "SEER Cancer Statistics Review 1975-2007," Tables 1.14 and 1.17, http://seer.cancer.gov/csr/1975_2007/results_merged/topic_lifetime_risk.pdf) For the 125,000 people in the affected area, the estimated lifetime incidence of cancer would thus be approximately 54,513 people, and the estimated lifetime deaths from cancer, 26,438. The attack would increase the lifetime incidence of cancer by 461 people, and lifetime deaths from cancer by 314. The Figure assumes no relocation, sheltering, or decontamination. All these actions would occur in the real world, significantly reducing cancer incidence and deaths caused by the attack.

Radioactive Materials and Sources

How large a source is required for an RDD, and what materials are most suitable? The Nuclear Regulatory Commission (NRC) has established thresholds for quantities of material requiring certain protective measures: "The theft or diversion of risk-significant quantities of radioactive materials could lead to their use in a radiological dispersal device (RDD) or a radiological exposure device (RED)."[277] **Table A-1** presents the risk-significant quantities of 16 materials that might be of use in an RDD. Note that these quantities are very small, often a fraction of a gram. These materials and quantities are from the International Atomic Energy Agency's Code of Conduct on the Safety and Security of Radioactive Sources, which that agency's Board of Governors approved in 2003 and which NRC helped prepare.[278]

---

[277] See Nuclear Regulatory Commission, "Physical Protection of Byproduct Material: Proposed Rule," 75 *Federal Register* 33902, June 15, 2010." for a brief discussion of REDs.

[278] International Atomic Energy Agency, *Code of Conduct on the Safety and Security of Radioactive Sources,* January 2004, http://www.iaea.org/Publications/Booklets/RadioactiveSources/radioactivesource.pdf.

Table A-1. Radionuclides and Quantities of Concern Regulated by NRC

Quantities Correspond to Category 2 Sources in IAEA Code of Conduct

Radionuclide	Quantity of Concern, in Units of ...			Threshold (Ci) to contaminate 1 square km assuming per-fect dispersion
	terabecquerels (TBq)	curies (Ci)	grams (g)	
Americium-241	0.6	16.22	4.73	78
Americium-241/beryllium	0.6	16.22	~4.73	~78
Californium-252	0.2	5.41	0.01	49
Curium-244	0.5	13.51	0.17	130
Cobalt-60	0.3	8.11	0.007	11
Cesium-137	1	27.03	0.31	42
Gadolinium-153	10	270.27	0.08	390
Iridium-192	0.8	21.62	0.002	100
Promethium-147	400	10810.81	11.66	410,000*
Plutonium-238	0.6	16.22	0.95	220
Plutonium-239/beryllium	0.6	16.22	16.22*	220*
Radium-226	0.4	10.81	10.93	13
Selenium-75	2	54.05	0.004	150
Strontium-90 (yttrium-90)	10	270.27	1.98	200
Thulium-170	200	5405.41	0.033*	2000
Ytterbium-169	3	81.08	0.003	600

Source: The list of radionuclides and the TBq column are from "Table 1: Radionuclides of Concern," in U.S. Nuclear Regulatory Commission, "Order Imposing Increased Controls (Effective Immediately)," EA-05-090, November 14, 2005, http://www.nrc.gov/security/byproduct/table1.pdf. (1 TBq = 27.027 Ci) NRC extracted the list and TBq column from International Atomic Energy Agency, "Code of Conduct on the Safety and Security of Radioactive Sources," Table 1, "Activities Corresponding to Thresholds of Categories," p. 16. Specific activity, used here to calculate grams, is from U.S. Department of Energy. Office of Environmental Management. "Table B.1. Characteristics of Important Radionuclides," http://www.orau.org/ptp/PTP%20Library/library/DOE/Misc/Table%20B_1_%20Characteristics%20of%20Important%20Radionuclides.htm. CRS calculated columns for Ci and g. Data for column, "Threshold (Ci) to contaminate 1 square km," are from Sandia National Laboratories, *Radioactive Material Downselection and Source Prioritization Methodology: A Sandia National Laboratories Study in Support of the Global Threat Reduction Initiative*, May 8, 2009, p. 40, "Threshold Quantities Comparison." This document is Official Use Only; these figures are unclassified when not associated with a specific weapon. William Rhodes of Sandia National Laboratories provided data for cells marked with an asterisk.

Notes: "Radionuclides of concern" are those for which, in the specified "quantities of concern," NRC requires enhanced security, such as access control, personnel security, and record-keeping. These quantities are Category 2 sources in the IAEA Code of Conduct. The threshold for Category 1 sources is 100 times that for Category 2 sources; the threshold for Category 3 sources is one tenth that for Category 2 sources. A quantity of concern is a very small amount. One ounce is 28.35 grams; many quantities of concern are less than 1 gram.

"Threshold to contaminate 1 square km" shows the amount of material, in curies, to contaminate that area to a level that a person in that area for a year would receive a dose of 2 rem in the first year after an attack, the EPA/FEMA protective action guide for relocation. NRC explained the rationale for the area chosen, 1 square km: "Given all the uncertainties, it was a criterion used that might represent significant economic losses, primarily from decontamination and disposal from cleanup efforts. The thresholds being used for significant [radiological exposure devices] and RDDs are the IAEA Code of Conduct Category 2 values." (Comments prepared by NRC, November 30, 2010.) The figures in this column assume perfectly even dispersion of material over the total area.

They are a useful metric for comparing the ability of different radionuclides to contaminate, but perfect dispersion would not occur in the real world. Further, the masses of material needed to produce this level of contamination would be somewhat higher than shown because materials used in commerce would not be pure.

For 14 of the 16 isotopes, the quantity of concern (in curies) in the center column is less than the amount of material (in curies) needed to contaminate 1 square km in the rightmost column. One of the two isotopes for which this is not the case, thulium-170, is very rare in commerce, and for the other, strontium-90, the difference between the two quantities is not great. Thus, protecting quantities of concern generally suffices to protect quantities that could be used to create a "significant" RDD.

The Code of Conduct uses TBq as the benchmark to define quantities of concern; CRS converted TBq to Ci. Entry for grams is obtained by dividing TBq by specific activity (expressed in TBq/gram). Entries in right two columns for strontium-90 (yttrium-90) are for strontium-90. Blank cells indicate data not available.

Rhodes notes that the figure for promethium-147 is so large because that isotope is "essentially a weak pure beta emitter." That is, curies measure the number of disintegrations per second, not energy emitted per disintegration. Since each disintegration of promethium-247 produces very little energy, and in a form of particles that travel only a short distance, it takes a large amount to contaminate 1 square km to the level that would produce the specified dose.

The IAEA decided that the code "should serve as guidance to States for—*inter alia*—the development and harmonization of policies, laws and regulations on the safety and security of radioactive sources."[279] For each radionuclide, the code lists three categories of radiation (expressed in curies and terabecquerels) and the threshold radiation value for each category based on potential to cause deterministic effects. Category 1 sources are those that, if not safely managed or securely protected, could cause permanent injury to someone who handled them for a few minutes, and death to someone who handled them unshielded for a few minutes to an hour. For Category 2 sources, the corresponding figures are minutes to hours and hours to days. Category 3 sources, if not safely managed or securely protected, could cause injury to someone handling them for some hours.[280] The Energy Policy Act of 2005 (P.L. 109-58, Section 651 (d)) mandates use of Category 1 or 2 sources as defined by the Code of Conduct as the basis for protecting radiation sources.

Separately, the National Nuclear Security Administration (NNSA) commissioned a study by Sandia National Laboratories to identify radionuclides suitable for use in an RDD.[281] Sandia started with all 3,715 nuclides discovered so far and eliminated all but 14 radionuclides plus nuclear reactor spent fuel.

The Code of Conduct, while nonbinding, sets worldwide standards for protection of radioactive sources. The United States adopted its categories to make its practice consistent with the code even though the Sandia study arrived at a slightly different list of radionuclides. The code urges all states to have an effective system of legislative and regulatory control of the specified radioactive sources.

The IAEA selected the radionuclides based on their availability, radioactivity, and other characteristics. Further, according to NRC, "Of the 16 radionuclides, only four are widely used in civilian applications in this country: Cobalt-60, cesium-137, iridium-192, and americium-241."[282] An expert panel highlighted the risk from cesium-137 chloride:

---

[279] International Atomic Energy Agency, *Code of Conduct on the Safety and Security of Radioactive Sources*, p. 2.
[280] Ibid., p. 15.
[281] *Radioactive Material Downselection and Source Prioritization Methodology*, A Sandia National Laboratories Study in Support of the Global Threat Reduction Initiative, May 8, 2009, pp. 4-15.
[282] "Prepared Statement of Robert J. Lewis," Director, Division of Materials Safety and State Agreements, Nuclear (continued...)

Because of its dispersibility, solubility, penetrating radiation, source activity, and presence across the United States in facilities such as hospitals, blood banks, and universities, many of which are located in large population centers, radioactive cesium chloride is a greater concern than other Category 1 and 2 sources for some attack scenarios. This concern is exacerbated by the lack of an avenue for permanent disposal of high-activity cesium radiation sources, which can result in disused cesium sources sitting in licensees' storage facilities. As such, these sources pose unique risks.[283]

Similarly, NRC stated:

CsCl [cesium chloride] sources comprise approximately 3% of the IAEA Category 1 and 2 quantity sources in the U.S. Many in the medical and scientific communities indicate that these CsCl sources are important due to their application in blood irradiation, bio-medical and industrial research, and calibration of instrumentation and dosimetry, especially for critical reactor and first responder equipment. ... The CsCl used in these applications is in a compressed powder form that is doubly-encapsulated in two stainless steel capsules to ensure safety and security in normal use. This physical form is used because of its high specific activity (gamma emission per unit volume) and manufacturability. However, the powder is highly soluble and dispersible, which presents security concerns.[284]

On the other hand, there are reasons for the use of cesium-137 chloride:

The widespread use of cesium chloride is a vital component of radiobiological and medical research and of clinical medicine ... Currently, and for the near future, there is no alternative to it in many applications. The [cesium-137 single-energy] spectrum has been the reference standard for radiobiological research for over 60 [years] and is the basis for national and international standards for dosimetry and instrument calibration; it cannot simply be replaced by x-rays. Indeed, any move away from using the [cesium-137] spectrum would necessitate years of repetition of impractical and fundamental radiobiological studies to redefine and verify another standard. Its elimination would impose great difficulties and financial hardship on clinical-medical applications.[285]

While the IAEA selected the thresholds in the Code of Conduct based on the potential to cause deterministic effects, these thresholds can also be used to calculate the relative effectiveness (as measured by area contaminated) of different materials when used in an RDD by showing how much material is needed to contaminate a specified area to a specified level. For example, under ideal conditions that could not be achieved in the real world, a Category 2 source of cobalt-60, 0.007 grams, could contaminate 0.74 square km (0.29 square miles) to the extent that people in that area could be expected to receive a dose of 2 rem in the first year following an attack or 0.5 rem in any succeeding year, the PAGs for which FEMA recommends relocating people from an area. In contrast, it would take 0.36 grams of cesium-137 (and a somewhat larger amount of cesium chloride) or 16.77 grams of americium-241 to contaminate the same area. Note that the

---

(...continued)

Regulatory Commission, in U.S. Congress. House. Committee on Homeland Security. Subcommittee on Emerging Threats, Cybersecurity, and Science and Technology, Status Report on Federal and Local Efforts to Secure Radiological Sources, field hearing, Brooklyn, NY, 111th Congress, 1st Session, serial no. 111-34, September 14, 2009, p. 21.

[283] National Research Council. *Radiation Source Use and Replacement, Abbreviated Version*, p. 7.

[284] Nuclear Regulatory Commission, "Request for Comments on the Draft Policy Statement on the Protection of Cesium-137 Chloride Sources and Notice of Public Meeting," 75 *Federal Register* 37486, June 29, 2010.

[285] Stephen Musolino, D. Thomas Coulter, and Hailu Tedla, "Cesium Chloride: Dispersibility or Security?," editorial, *Health Physics,* May 2011, vol. 100, no. 5, p. 459.

amounts of material in the foregoing examples are less than 1 ounce, and that a dose of 2 rem/year would not cause deterministic effects.

Terrorists could not manufacture material of greatest concern for use in an RDD because it is made in nuclear reactors. Some such materials are specially manufactured by bombarding stable (nonradioactive) atoms with neutrons produced by nuclear reactors, increasing the number of neutrons in the nucleus. In this way, stable cobalt-59, with 32 neutrons, is transformed into radioactive cobalt-60, with 33. Other radionuclides are byproducts of a nuclear reactor. When uranium fissions in a reactor, two of the many resulting radionuclides are cesium-137 and strontium-90, which are chemically separated from spent fuel.[286] Only a few reactors worldwide produce cobalt-60, cesium-137, and some other radionuclides for commercial sale. For example, "Separated radioactive cesium sold internationally is produced only by the Production Association Mayak (PA Mayak), in the Chelyabinsk region of Russia and sold through the U.K.-based company, REVISS."[287]

As a result, terrorists would have to obtain this material through theft, purchase, or transfer from sympathetic insiders. Most likely, they would try to obtain "sealed" sources, such as shown in **Figure A-6**. Sealed sources, a common form in which radioactive material is sold, enclose radioactive material in a metal capsule to make sure it does not leak and contaminate people or the environment. Sealed sources have many beneficial uses. They treat cancers,[288] irradiate food,[289] monitor wells for oil,[290] have military applications,[291] create radiographs (x-ray-like images) for inspecting cargo containers,[292] and are used in research.[293] As a result of this utility, millions are in use worldwide. They vary widely in number of curies. Some food irradiators have millions of curies; blood irradiators have several thousand curies; and many, such as household smoke detectors, have a tiny fraction of a curie. The latter do not pose a terrorist threat. Because of the threat and wide distribution of risk-significant sources, the United States and other countries have taken steps, discussed in the next section, to protect these sources.

Radioisotopic thermal generators (RTGs) in Russia are of special concern. These devices, powered by several thousand curies of strontium-90, produce heat that is converted to electricity

---

[286] See National Research Council. Division on Earth and Life Studies. Nuclear and Radiation Studies Board. Committee on Radiation Source Use and Replacement, *Radiation Source Use and Replacement, Abbreviated Version*, Washington, DC, 2008, pp. 26, 27, 30, 33, http://www.nap.edu/catalog.php?record_id=11976.

[287] Ibid., p. 27.

[288] U.S. Department of Health and Human Services. National Institutes of Health. National Cancer Institute. "Radiation Therapy for Cancer: Questions and Answers," http://www.cancer.gov/cancertopics/factsheet/Therapy/radiation.

[289] U.S. Environmental Protection Agency. "Food Irradiation," http://www.epa.gov/radiation/sources/food_irrad.html.

[290] Falah Abu-Jarad, "The Application of Radiation Sources in the Oil and Gas Industry and Shortages in Their Services," *Atoms for Peace*, vol. 2, no. 4 (2009), pp. 338-349, http://inderscience.metapress.com/app/home/contribution.asp?referrer=parent&backto=issue,3,8;journal,3,9;linkingpublicationresults,1:119867,1.

[291] Radiation Source Protection and Security Task Force, report, August 15, 2006, section "The IAEA [International Atomic Energy Agency] Code of Conduct," http://hps.org/govtrelations/documents/nrc_source_taskforce_execsummary.pdf.

[292] For example, the Rapiscan GaRDS Mobile cargo and vehicle inspection system uses cobalt-60 as its gamma-ray source. Rapiscan Systems, "Rapiscan GaRDS Mobile," data sheet, p. 2, http://www.rapiscansystems.com/datasheets/Rapiscan_GaRDSMobile_Screen.pdf.

[293] For example, see U.S. Nuclear Regulatory Commission. Office of Public Affairs. "Safety and Security of Cesium-137 Chloride Sealed Sources, Remarks by The Honorable Peter B. Lyons, Commissioner, U.S. Nuclear Regulatory Commission, [at] Workshop on the Security and Continued Use of Cesium-137 Chloride Sources, Rockville, MD, September 29, 2008," no. S-08-036, http://adamswebsearch2.nrc.gov/idmws/doccontent.dll?library=PU_ADAMS^PBNTAD01&ID=082740186.

---

for use at remote locations, such as to power lighthouses.[294] A 2007 paper by NNSA staff said, "these [Russian] RTGs likely represent the largest unsecured quantity of radiological material in the world."[295] To counter the threat of terrorists taking RTGs for use in an RDD, the United States, Russia, Norway, France, and other countries have been securing these devices. (See "**G8 Global Partnership:**.") NNSA expects that by the end of FY2011, 646 of 851 RTGs will have been recovered.[296]

Figure A-6. A Sealed Source

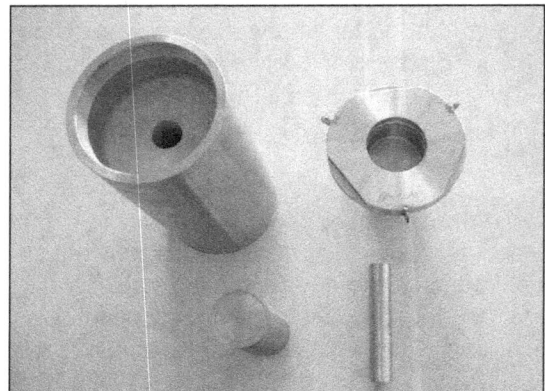

Source: International Atomic Energy Agency

Notes: This figure shows a thin cylinder of radioactive material and its protective capsule.

Might uranium or plutonium, the essential fuels of nuclear weapons, be used in an RDD? Terrorists could use a relatively innocuous radioactive material like uranium in an RDD in an attempt to create panic, but authorities would surely take steps to counter panic, so the net result is unknown. However, technical experts rarely if ever consider uranium as an RDD material because the amount of radiation emitted per gram is extremely small, most of its gamma rays are of relatively low energy,[297] and it poses less of a biological hazard than plutonium. Plutonium could be used in an RDD because of the biological hazards from alpha particles if inhaled. However, a terrorist group seeking materials for an RDD would probably find it easier to obtain radionuclides with common industrial uses, a terrorist group seeking to build a nuclear bomb would probably try to acquire uranium highly enriched in isotope 235 ("highly enriched uranium") rather than plutonium because only the former can be used in the simplest type of nuclear bomb, and a terrorist group seeking to build a nuclear bomb using plutonium would probably not squander any plutonium it acquired on an RDD. On the other hand, spent nuclear fuel, a highly radioactive mixture of many radionuclides including uranium and plutonium, could be used in an RDD.

---

[294] Cristina Chuen, "Radiological Materials in Russia," Nuclear Threat Initiative, July 2004, http://www.nti.org/e_research/e3_51a html.

[295] Jill Zubarev and Garry Tittemore, Office of Global Threat Reduction, National Nuclear Security Administration, Department of Energy, "The Global Threat Reduction Initiative: Enhancing Radiological Security in the Russian Federation," c. 2007, p. 3, http://www.iaea.org/OurWork/ST/NE/NEFW/CEG/documents/ws052007_15E.pdf.

[296] U.S. Department of Energy. Office of Chief Financial Officer. *FY 2011 Congressional Budget Request.* volume 1, National Nuclear Security Administration, DOE/CF-0047, February 2010, p. 443, http://www.cfo.doe.gov/budget/11budget/Content/Volume%201.pdf.

[297] While uranium-232 emits a gamma ray of very high energy (2,614 keV), it is present only in trace amounts in HEU, 100 parts per trillion. Bernard Phlips et al., "Comparison of Shielded Uranium Passive Gamma-Ray Detection Methods," *Proceedings of SPIE,* vol. 6213 62130H-2. Uranium-232 is not present in nature, and is present only in uranium that has been through a nuclear reactor.

Appendix B. Some U.S. Vulnerabilities to RDDs

Table B-1. Some U.S. vulnerabilities to RDDs based on 2009 testimony of Kenneth Sheely, NNSA, updated with 2010 comments by NNSA

Statement	Vulnerability
NNSA's Global Threat Reduction Initiative (GTRI) has begun installing delay mechanisms for a type of radiological source of high concern, but completion is not slated until 2016: "A study by the National Academy of Sciences identified Cesium Chloride (CsCl) as posing a greater concern than the other radionuclides because it is widely used in significant quantities and is soluble and dispersible. … The key finding of [another] study was that the radioactive sources within self-shielded cesium irradiators could be extracted more quickly than initially thought." (pp. 13-14)	"As of August 31, 2009 IDD kits have been installed on 32 irradiators. The remaining 808 irradiators can be hardened by fiscal year 2016. The implementation schedule is primarily constrained by human resource needs, scheduling complexities, and budget." (p. 16) An IDD is a cesium chloride irradiator in-device delay, a mechanism retrofitted into existing irradiators or designed into new ones to make it "orders of magnitude more difficult for an adversary to illicitly access and steal the radiological source." (p. 15) As of February 2011, GTRI had installed IDDs on 238 of more than 800 cesium irradiators. In October 2010, NNSA stated that program completion was scheduled by FY2016.
Many sources are in open environments: "Radiological sources are located at thousands of civilian sites across the United States and around the world." (p. 14)	"Medical, university, and research facilities are, by nature and design, 'open' environments that allow a larger set of people access to these materials. These types of facilities are more difficult to secure than isolated military installations or nuclear power plants which are designed to be closed to all but a very limited number of personnel." (p. 14)
The number of unwanted sources in long-term storage is growing: "At present, only 14 States in the United States have access to commercial disposal for sealed sources (with the exception of Ra-226 sources which have a commercial disposal pathway in all 50 States). With the decline in commercial disposal options, GTRI has seen an increase in the number of sources being registered as excess and unwanted." (p. 15)	"GTRI has found that without disposal access, source owners have no option other than long-term storage, which increases the vulnerability of [a source] becoming lost or forgotten." (p. 15) So, the number of excess and unwanted sources is growing, which increases vulnerability, and the time for which they are stored is growing, which further increases vulnerability. This number continues to increase even though GTRI, as of February 2011, had recovered over 27,000 disused and unwanted sources.
Alarm response capability at many facilities is questionable: "At military facilities and nuclear power plants, there are highly-trained operators who are located in hardened central alarm stations (CAS) who monitor the detection devices 24/7. These detection alarms are hardwired into the CAS and if an alarm goes off or the power is turned off, there is nearly 100 percent probability that the CAS operator will receive the alarm and immediately notify the large, well-trained, well-armed on-site response team as to the exact location and condition causing the alarm." (p. 16)	"In comparison, at many hospitals or universities, the alarms are not monitored by well-trained CAS operators sitting in a secure location. The alarms are instead sent to normal facility employees or unarmed guards on-site. Assuming the adversary hasn't already neutralized these lightly-armed on-site personnel, the emergency call will be handled by a 9–1–1 operator who will have little understanding of what an irradiator is or why cesium warrants an emergency response. The chances that a large, well-trained, well-armed off-site response will arrive in time from local law enforce[ment] under these conditions is greatly reduced due to the limited amount of reliable transmission of alarms." (p. 16)

Statement	Vulnerability
GTRI will not complete deployment of technology to counter insider threat until FY2019: "The greatest potential threat at hospitals and universities is that an insider could be the guard or employee who is on duty during off-hours and merely turns off or ignores the alarms. No one will know the source is gone until the next shift begins perhaps 12 hours or more later." (p. 16)	"GTRI prioritizes which sites receive voluntary security enhancements ... GTRI estimates that there are about 2,200 buildings in the United States that house IAEA Category I or II levels of radiological materials. As of August 31, 2009, 37 buildings have been completed with the remaining buildings to be complete by fiscal year 2016." (p. 17) As of February 2011, GTRI had revised the number of "vulnerable buildings ... with high priority radioactive material in the United States" to more than 2,700, had completed security upgrades at 251 of them, and was "aiming" for completion by 2025.
GTRI has trained a limited number of first responders: "The most important aspect of any security system is a timely, well-equipped, well-trained response team of appropriate size to interrupt and neutralize the adversary before they gain access to the radioactive source. GTRI has therefore made a focused effort to provide security personnel and local law enforcement with the tools and training needed to adequately respond to a security incident. Most on-site guards at facilities with radioactive sources are not armed or large enough force strength to neutralize the threat. Therefore, the key responders are often off-site local law enforcement. Unfortunately, many local law enforcement officials are not made aware of the nature of the material which is in use at hospitals, blood banks, universities, oil fields, and manufacturing plants in their jurisdiction. It is important for their safety, and the safety of their communities, that they receive proper training about radiological sources. To ensure that both on-site and offsite responders understand how to respond to enhanced security system alarms, GTRI has developed an alarm response training course run by the Y–12 National Security Complex in Oak Ridge, TN." (p. 17)	"As of August 31, 2009 we have conducted 6 training courses for 175 responders from 7 cities." (p. 17) As of September 2010, GTRI had completed 23 alarm response training courses for over 800 students from 81 sites in 21 states. As of February 2011, the course had trained 1,118 local law enforcement officers. But in 2009, there were 706,886 law enforcement officers and 314,570 law enforcement civilians in the United States. (note 1) Thus GTRI had provided its alarm response training course to a tiny fraction of U.S. law enforcement employees. On the other hand, not every U.S. jurisdiction has high-activity radioactive sources, and not every local law enforcement officer in jurisdictions with such sources is responsible for responding to alarms from those facilities. NNSA indicated in October 2010 that its "training is not meant to directly cover every officer from every responding [local law enforcement agency]. The goal is to impart the knowledge necessary to the correct people who can take this experience back to their agencies and share it or integrate it into their training programs."
GTRI has offered tabletop exercises [TTX] to a limited number of civilian sites: "As the capstone of GTRI's voluntary security enhancement support, GTRI has partnered with NNSA's Office of the Under Secretary for Counterterrorism and the FBI's Weapons of Mass Destruction Directorate to provide table top exercises at select nuclear and radiological sites. The purpose is to provide a no-fault, site-specific scenario where senior managers from various Federal, State, and municipal organizations can exercise their crisis management and consequence management skills in response to a terrorist incident." (p. 17)	"As of August 31, 2009 we have conducted 3 TTXs at facilities located in Honolulu, HI, Philadelphia, PA, and Manhattan, KS. A fourth TTX was recently completed in Houston, TX in early September." (p. 17) NNSA indicated that as of September 2010, GTRI had conducted TTXs at 10 sites. The number of these exercises is far less than the number of sites that might benefit from them. NNSA commented in October 2010 that "TTX are not needed for every site we provide enhancements to. TTXs are strategically planned based on location each year. TTX are conducted at an individual site, but personnel from sites in the surrounding area are also invited to observe and learn lessons that may translate back to their facilities. Furthermore, LLEA in an individual city are responsible for all of the sites in that city so multiple TTXs in one city may be overwhelming for these agencies and would provide a diminishing returns. GTRI generally gets the most 'bang for the buck' in large metropolitan areas where there is one response force for many sites."

Statement	Vulnerability
Technology to further reduce vulnerability of sources in transit may be years from deployment. "Radioactive sealed sources may be at their most vulnerable when in transit. Recognizing this, GTRI has begun to implement security upgrades beyond regulatory requirements on our own source recovery shipments. GTRI has undertaken a number of pilot projects testing existing security devices/systems and has found that there is not a commercially available system that meets all our needs. Therefore, we are putting the best available compatible equipment on our vehicles and will continue to improve our system as additional technology advances are made. Because we are looking for a system(s) that private industry can adopt, we are working with the DHS-led interagency group and directly with some in industry to demonstrate a prototype system using the best available devices. GTRI is offering industry a test bed to evaluate their devices for compatibility and capability to operate in the harsh transit environment, (e.g., heat, cold, jarring, etc)." (pp. 17-18)	If transportation security technology does not meet all GTRI's own needs for transporting recovered sealed sources, it presumably does not meet all the needs for secure commercial transport of such sources. The prototype systems demonstrated use commercial off-the-shelf equipment. Nonetheless, the process of demonstrating these systems, refining them so they are suitable for operating in the transit environment, and then producing and deploying them may take years, so this transportation vulnerability is not likely to be fully addressed for some time.

Source: Except as indicated, statements are from "Prepared Statement of Kenneth Sheely," Associate Assistant Deputy Administrator for Global Threat Reduction, National Nuclear Security Administration, Department of Energy, in U.S. Congress. House. Committee on Homeland Security. Subcommittee on Emerging Threats, Cybersecurity, and Science and Technology, *Status Report on Federal and Local Efforts to Secure Radiological Sources,* field hearing,, Brooklyn, NY, 111th Congress, 1st Session, serial no. 111-34, September 14, 2009, http://www.gpo.gov/fdsys/pkg/CHRG-111hhrg54223/pdf/CHRG-111hhrg54223.pdf. Page numbers refer to pages in this hearing. NNSA provided updates for 2010, email, October 14, 2010. Updates for February 2011 are from U.S. Department of Energy. National Nuclear Security Administration. "NNSA: Securing Domestic Radioactive Material," fact sheet, February 1, 2011, p. 2. Note 1: U.S. Department of Justice. Federal Bureau of Investigation. *Crime in the United States, 2009,* Table 74, Full-Time Law Enforcement Employees by Population Group, Percent Male and Female, 2009, http://www.fbi.gov/about-us/cjis/ucr/crime-in-the-u.s/2009/cius2009/?searchterm=crime%20in%20the%20united%20states%202009.

sajdfklsjadflksad;fkls;adkfl;ksad

Author Contact Information

Jonathan Medalia
Specialist in Nuclear Weapons Policy
jmedalia@crs.loc.gov, 7-7632